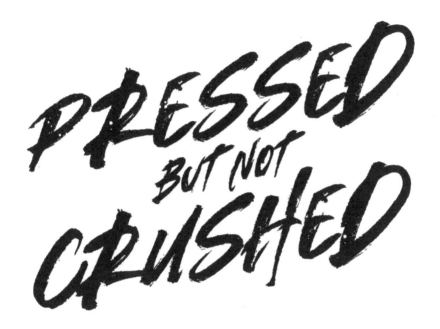

Strategies for Overcoming
in the Midst of Spiritual Warfare

CASSANDRA BELLEVUE

possible, but it's because he is terrified of the damage that the calling on your life is intended to do to his plans.

I pray over you the same prayer I pray over my own life. I pray that you make the enemy regret the day he ever tried you, challenged you, and decided to take steps to sabotage your life. May your future and destiny deliver such a blow to the kingdom of darkness that it will never fully recover. I encourage you to be unapologetically you and walk in an anointing like King David – a mighty man after God's own heart. May you allow Papa God to turn your pressing around to produce the good work that's needed in your life. I'm rooting for you, KAD! Love, "Philly."

ACKNOWLEDGEMENTS

Back in the beginning of 2018, I had a burning message in my heart. In order to get it out of my system I wrote an article/blog post (or so I thought). After writing it, I felt like the Lord told me to send it to two people to read it: my friends Rhonda Fleming and Tasha McAlpine. I was thinking, "Whaaaaat!?" It felt so vulnerable. "Let people read it? Seriously?" I know I just said I wrote an "article" or "blog post" but I didn't have a blog or any newspapers I was connected to. I just typed it all out because I needed it out of my system! LOL!

Rhonda, when the Lord told me to send what turned out to be Chapter 2 of this book to you, I was shaking in my boots. "But she's a real editor, God! She doesn't have time to be reading my fake articles!" My friend, I want you to know you were extremely instrumental in laying out the strategy for this book. Although God had already prophesied to me through many people that I'd someday write a book, I don't know how seriously I was taking it. But when you replied back to me after reading it,

> "Cassandra,
>
> Wow!!!
>
> First . . . your writing is exquisite!! Seriously, girl. Keep writing!! It is engaging. It flows. It is inspiring. It is encouraging. It is challenging (in a personal, spiritual way). So . . . it's ~3K words. Ten 'chapters' like that and you have a 100-page book. Just so you know."

I read those last lines and I knew I'd been set up by Holy Spirit! Haha! To this Type A personality, it made that pipe dream seem doable and I am forever grateful to you. The entire time I was writing it, my tangible goal was to hit 30K words and at least 10 chapters. I could hear you cheering me on all along the way. When I completed the book on 8/8/20 I didn't even have to think twice about who I'd be hiring to edit it. I love you, friend! Thank you for championing me! I am forever grateful for you and our friendship!

Tasha, I was silently hoping you wouldn't even read it when I sent it to you back in 2018! I knew Law School had left you "allergic" to reading, but you supported me so well! Haha! I know you're a straight shooter without a trace of a flattering tongue. So when you said you wanted to quote some of my sentences from the article on social media, I was floored, tickled, and humbled all at the same time. Thank you, friend.

You have spent over 10 years witnessing and walking this "pressed but not crushed" message with me. Oh how precious it has been having someone to labor, war, and intercede with these last 10 years.

A huge shout out to Fox & Hound Design for creating the book cover! I have zero design experience, background, or gifting. Coming up with a book cover design was an extremely daunting and overwhelming task. After a simple 10-minute conversation with Coty and Katie Sloan with Fox and Hound, they were able to capture the exact feel and intensity I wanted the book cover to inspire. You both are anointed and a gift from God. I'm thankful for our friendship and the privilege and honor to collaborate with you. I'll be back for the next book cover!

CONTENTS

CHAPTER 1

DTR – Defining the Relationship

Several years ago, a childhood friend asked me a question. It was a simple question, but one I didn't have an immediate answer for. Having witnessed me go through a ton of hardships and disappointments over the 20+ years we had been friends, she was curious. This particular day she had listened attentively as I shared the latest obstacle I was battling. When I was done she asked, "Cassandra, what keeps you going? What keeps you fighting and feeling hopeful? I don't know how you do it."

I'd never been asked that before. Now that I was put on the spot, I scrambled to come up with an answer. I almost answered with the same answer you gave to every question you got asked in Sunday School as a kid: "JESUS!" Haha! However, I knew she was asking for practical insight to help her with some obstacles she was battling. After a moment of silence, I gave her some tips, tools, and disciplines I had used and practiced over the last few years. I ended my response with, "Yeah, other than those things, I don't really know how to answer that loaded question."

Her response was, "Well, you should figure it out. And when you do, you need to write a book about it." We both laughed. Well, lo and behold, here I am almost 11 years later doing just that.

Jesus said in John 16:33, "I have said these things to you, that in me you may have peace. In this world, you will have tribulation. But take heart; I have overcome the world."

If you are a believer, I hope the person who helped lead you to Christ didn't feed you a bunch of lines about how perfectly euphoric your life was going to be after Jesus. I talked to a new believer recently and I specifically told them, "Well, now that you've aligned with Christ, you have a lifelong enemy who's not happy with you. He's going to attempt to sabotage your destiny, but you are more than a conqueror through Christ Jesus." They looked at me a little terrified! But you know what? I would rather set proper expectations than try to oversell someone through wrong expectations and mindsets.

If you are not yet a believer (having made Jesus Christ Lord of your life) but find yourself reading this book ... heads up! Holy Spirit is setting you up! Just letting you know. Apparently, He wants your expectations to be set correctly from the start. He wants you to be aware and avoid some of the enemy's traps so you can live victoriously. Buckle up and enjoy!

Before I go any further, I want to say this: Giving my life to Christ is single handedly *the best* decision I've ever made in my entire life. If I had to do it all over, I'd make the same decision over and over again. I have never once regretted it. And one of my biggest passions is to encourage and champion people in their own walk with God.

Do you know what the first thing the church I was saved in recommended new believers start doing right off the bat? Get in the Word! Read the Bible. Why? Because the Word of God *is* the training manual for this Christian walk. More importantly, it is the source of our *POWER*! It's one of our God-given weapons we're to use to overcome! Have you ever noticed that when the Apostle Paul wrote about the "Armor of God" in Ephesians, he only lists *one* offensive weapon? Everything else is defensive or protective gear. Let's take a look:

> Finally, be strong in the Lord and in his mighty power. Put on the full armor of God, so that you can take your stand against the devil's schemes. For our struggle is not against flesh and

blood, but against the rulers, against the authorities, against the powers of this dark world and against the spiritual forces of evil in the heavenly realms. Therefore put on the full armor of God, so that when the day of evil comes, you may be able to stand your ground, and after you have done everything, to stand. Stand firm then, with the belt of truth buckled around your waist, with the breastplate of righteousness in place, and with your feet fitted with the readiness that comes from the gospel of peace. In addition to all this, take up the shield of faith, with which you can extinguish all the flaming arrows of the evil one. Take the helmet of salvation and the sword of the Spirit, which is the word of God. And pray in the Spirit on all occasions with all kinds of prayers and requests. With this in mind, be alert and always keep on praying for all the Lord's people. - Ephesians 6:10–18

We get *one* offensive weapon. It's a sword and it's the WORD - the Word of God! The living and breathing Word of God! It's not a dry history book we read for informational purposes. It's alive, active, living, and breathing! This means when you need a strategy for an obstacle you're dealing with, the Bible has your solution. When you are having the worst day ever, there are powerful words of encouragement found in the Bible that can catapult you into a place of hope and even joy! What I'm getting at is that the Bible contains real life solutions and applications.

So, by now you may be thinking, "What did I get myself into reading this book? Warfare!? Armor!? A sabotaging enemy!? Tribulation in life!?" And that was all before you even got out of Chapter 1. Just consider this the best DTR ever. Full disclosure. HAHA! I mean, the title of my book alone would make most people run for the hills. The fact that you made it this far probably means God has prepared you for this journey with me - a sister in Christ who's not afraid to keep it 100% authentic concerning the not-so-chipper seasons of life.

Second Corinthians 4:8 says, "We are pressed on every side by troubles, but we are not crushed. We are perplexed, but not driven to despair."

Continue reading and find out how it's possible to be pressed but not crushed as you pursue God and His will for your life with your entire heart, soul, and mind. So, with that, as my son would say, "LET'S GOOOOOOOOO!"

CHAPTER 2

2017: The Year of Victory

W hen the Hebrew year 5777 kicked off, 2017 for the rest of the world, I was certain it would be my year of breakthrough. To hear the prophetic voices from multiple streams tell it, this was our year of *VICTORY*! I believed the prophets and I was ready… BEYOND READY. I'd been waiting a LONG TIME for change. Good change! Exciting change! ACTUAL BREAKTHROUGH!

But we weren't even a full month into 2017 when life dealt me a major blow. The fact that it came from someone I was in the process of reconciling with, someone who had convinced me that it was time to trust them again, had an extremely brutal effect on my soul. In this walk with Papa God, there have been moments when I've felt like I had to remind Him that I'm not Jesus, and this was one of those moments.

Forgive 70 X 7 times? (Matthew 18:21-22). I'd done that. Love your enemies? I'd done that. To the point where I had a couple of close friends tell me they could never do what they were watching me do. Some admitted to me that they prayed God would never ask them to walk through what they'd seen me walk through. Yet, it felt like the hits just kept on coming in this one particular area of my life. I felt duped, played, and what hurt me the most is God just seemed to allow this "grace grower" to take advantage of me time and time again. The victorious 2017 felt like a sham already.

Let's fast forward to the last month of 2017.

It was a Friday night and I was planning on going to a service at one of my favorite churches in the Metro Atlanta area. That night they would be offering personal prophetic ministry to everyone in attendance. Say no more! I planned to be there. Anyone who knows me knows I treasure my prophetic words. I record them, type them out, meditate on them, war with them, and refer to them over and over. I believe in warring over your prophetic words and partnering with the Lord to see them come to fruition. This special service would be starting in about an hour. I knew it would take me 30 minutes to get there and I was simply waiting for my phone to charge so I could head out. As I was waiting, I felt the Holy Spirit prompting me to ask Him if I was even supposed to be going to that service. Hmmmmm. When I asked, I clearly heard, "No."

Really, God? I mean, what could be bad about going to a church service? However, over the years I've learned the principle of *Good vs. God*. I once heard an excellent teaching from John Bevere concerning this concept. You may want to check it out. Just because something is "good" doesn't mean it's God's will for you. So, after asking Him the same question seven times (LOL, I had to make sure I wasn't being duped by the enemy), I conceded.

Now, finding myself having to recalibrate my plans, I wondered what I was *supposed* to be doing that night? I immediately heard, "Go to the movies." I laughed out loud. The movies!? I didn't even know what movies were out, but after a quick internet search, I was off for a double feature. First up, *The Greatest Showman*! Followed by *Pitch Perfect 3*! With my musical theater background, you'd think it natural that I would gravitate toward those two shows. However, I really did feel led to select them. I also felt very strongly that God would meet me there, at the theater, as crazy as that may sound to some people.

The Greatest Showman stirred me to my core. The theme of dreaming to attain what seems impossible, the struggle of the outcasts and the underdogs, the conflict in relationships. I could relate to all of it on a very personal and painful level. The overarching theme of pushing until your dream is realized and never giving up had me floating out of the theater I was so pumped up. I had a new lease on life. I felt refreshed! I felt revived! I felt hopeful about all the promises God had spoken over me all over again.

Next up, *Pitch Perfect 3*. I have thoroughly enjoyed this series. Once again, with my musical theater passion, that fact isn't surprising. The *a cappella* performances, the humor, and the storyline all spoke to me.

I can't remember the moment it happened, or during which movie I had the encounter, but God showed up. I felt Papa say to me, "You know, 2017 really was your year of victory." Luckily, I wasn't eating or drinking anything because I probably would have spit most of it out while trying not to choke. "VICTORY?! REALLY!? How so?" In reviewing 2017, my mind gravitated toward all the lies, betrayal, and disappointment it had delivered to me. It was an emotional year, and not in a good way.

Sidebar. Can I just say I love the voice of the Father? He really is a good Dad. He meets us where we are and speaks to the deepest longings, sorrows, dreams, desires, and disappointments with the most heartfelt love and compassion. If you don't know Him, get to know Him. He's nothing like anyone has ever described because he caters to us individually. How you experience Papa God will be unique to you and the very best part of your life.

I pondered what He just spoke to me, "You know, 2017 really was your year of victory." I've been walking with Him long enough to know not to ever doubt what He says. This was an invitation to align with Him and His perspective. Sometimes, in order to come into alignment with truth, we're required to take a step back and go on a detour. I began reviewing 2017 in my mind. The first review was pretty shallow to be honest. I call it the Mountain Top Review. What were the best things (visibly) that happened to me this year? Hmmmmm. Still in the same job. Still in debt. Still on meds. Still dealing with what Graham Cooke calls "Grace Growers," aka difficult people/relationships. I couldn't follow God's logic, but I was determined to find the truth in what He was speaking to my heart.

It was time for a deeper review. I started tracking through 2017 month by month. January – HORRIBLY BLINDSIDED BY BETRAYAL – AGAIN. February – "Forced" to go to a women's retreat I didn't want to go to. And then the "aha" moment settled in. Back in January I felt the Holy Spirit prompting me to attend a February women's retreat that I had no desire to go to. I couldn't even understand why He wanted me to attend so badly. When I kept arguing, He simply said, "I just need you to be there." I assumed there would be something for me to *do* there, so I signed up. It's not that I minded the people or the theme of the retreat itself. I just lacked understanding of what my purpose would be there. That retreat turned out to be the most pivotal moment of my 2017.

It's hard to explain in words what transpired there. I mean, I attended all the corporate sessions and small group breakout sessions. Things were great! I made some new friends and even connected with some awesome intercessors. However, there was a deeper layer of work being done in me than what was happening on the surface. Although I was sitting in a session, hearing the speaker, agreeing with her bullet points, grateful for her testimony, it's like a second speaker/message/testimony was being poured into my spirit. I remember explaining it to a friend. I told her, "I was at a retreat, but it's like a separate, deeper, more underlying retreat was happening between just Holy Spirit and me … alone."

While in that corporate setting, Papa was speaking to me, preaching to me, exhorting me, and refreshing me in the areas of life that had become so draining. Have you ever faced a situation SO unbelievable that your brain just gets stuck in this "processing" mode? It's like your brain and heart say, "Please stand by while we process this craziness." Your mind tries "rebooting" your hardware time and time again, however, you wind up getting stuck in the same place every time. The triggered pain is happening so often it becomes your everyday reality, your new normal. Somehow, most likely by the grace of God, you don't lose your mind in the process.

I realized I was stuck. I was stuck "hoping for the best," "trusting without boundaries," "pouring out everything I had while getting scraps in return," "being taken advantage of while requiring no explanation." It's a basic fact of life, you cannot continue pouring out without being replenished and expect to be well in the end. But that was the crazy cycle I was stuck in.

That February, at that retreat, I surrendered and laid down all my pain before the Lord. I laid down all my expectations, too. I finally gave Him the main area of my life where I had been spinning my wheels and getting nowhere. This particular area of my life was one where I felt like I'd been sitting in a parked car … *for over a decade*! I kept expecting that car to start up at any minute. Then I would experience moments of hitting rock bottom when my situation didn't improve. It would come in waves.

That weekend in February, God invited me to recalibrate and step into a new mindset and outlook. That weekend, I stepped out of the parked car and moved on with my life. You know when you're driving with your GPS on and you approach an accident or make a wrong turn it will say, "Re-routing" or "Re-calibrating." I decided it was time to re-route! Maybe it's because I'd been mourning in that parked car for over a decade, but somehow, I was able to exit without much fanfare or emotion. It was like the Lord was standing outside my car window, peering in, with His hand out, saying, "Are you ready to get out now?" I'd already wasted enough of my life, emotions, and energy bemoaning how unfair the circumstances were. It's like I looked over at Him and said, "Yes, please." I opened the door, handed the situation to Him, and from that point on, my reality changed.

Nothing changed physically, but mentally and emotionally *everything* changed. I already knew all the behaviors that needed to change. MY behavior. MY response to things. MY expectations had to change. I already knew what I needed to do to move forward. I guess you could say it was the most anti-climactic breakthrough I've ever experienced. However, the results were probably some of the most life-changing.

Something major shifted for me when I stepped out of that "car." There was a windfall of many other unexpected mindsets that I was set free from, in tandem. I'll share one as an example. I tend to have no patience for flaky people. I know that this stems from personal wounds of being discounted and rejected by key people in my childhood and for most of my 20s. When you grow up being treated like a second-class citizen because you're different, you long for a home base, as well as people you consider "home." So, it would trigger me when people would make plans with me and just fail to show up, or when people would make plans and nonchalantly cancel last minute.

Example: You have two tickets to a show at a local theater. A person expresses interest and asks you to reserve that ticket for them. You oblige with the understanding that they will attend the show and also compensate you for the ticket.

Two days before the show you unexpectedly run into said person and they very flippantly tell you, "Oh, by the way, I can't go. I got invited to another event and I really want to go to that." OR "I'm just not feeling it. I'm tired so I'm going to rest for the next few days." Now, sure, that would annoy many people. But for someone like me who had a deep wound in that area, it becomes something more than a flaky person doing what they do. You get hammered with feelings of rejection and the lack of importance you hold in that person's life – especially if this is someone who means a lot to you.

As I reviewed 2017 through the eyes of Holy Spirit, I realized I had experienced several flaky incidents over the year. Some that even put me at a loss financially. However, this year I didn't react the same way I would have in the past. Instead, I had started putting people into categories:

A. Reliable/Trustworthy
B. Proceed with caution
C. Flaky/Avoid making plans at all costs

This is called setting boundaries. In the past, the broken agreement would have been all about me! I would get angry, wondering how they could do that to me. Then the thoughts would migrate to "What's wrong with me?" Now, hallelujah, I'm able to simply put each person in a category when it comes to making plans and move on with my life. Next time they approach me with plans, I will "hold it lightly" with an "if-it-happens-then-cool" mindset. However, I definitely will not make plans with them if it could put me in a bad situation should they cancel again.

The new me actually became grateful for these experiences! I actually became *grateful* to learn what type of people I was dealing with. This helped me to determine how to proceed in the future. It was such a simple but life-changing shift in mindset. Very liberating to say the least. You can say I stopped getting hurt by the actions of others, realizing it said more about their own character than me as a person.

There was a song from *The Greatest Showman* that resonated with me on a very deep and personal level. The song is called "This is Me" and it's sung by the outcasts of the society portrayed in the movie. The entire song became my anthem for 2018. One line talks about being assaulted by a round of bullets – the words and actions of others. The singer expresses how she considers herself invincible because she will not allow those bullets to sink in and do her any harm. I realized that beginning in 2017, the *bullets* could no longer penetrate me!

That year some pretty scandalous stuff was exposed within my family. And that's putting it mildly. When I shared some of the details with a friend, I had to laugh realizing she was more shaken by it than I was. I haven't become numb or desensitized and I haven't become uncaring. What I have become is someone who rolls with the punches and doesn't let the baggage of others drag me down. I've become someone who refuses to allow the undermining of others determine my worth and value. Only Abba Father can determine my worth! How someone treats me says more about them than me. I've learned that it's okay to set boundaries with people because, if you don't, the leeches will keep coming back. Should that happen, at the end of the day, you'll have no one to blame but yourself.

There are shameless people in this world who only care about themselves. The fix isn't to become a narcissist like them. The solution is to honor yourself with self-care and boundaries while continuing to love like Christ and follow His lead. He hasn't called us to be doormats and punching bags. In 2 Corinthians 12:9 He promised, "My grace is all you need. My power works best in weakness." And then Paul goes on to remind us, "So now I am glad to boast about my weaknesses, so that the power of Christ can work through me." And boy did His power hit me in a fresh new way! I love that! We can come out of difficult and painful experiences without bitterness and without feeling defeated. His power is our portion and available to us whenever we need it! He's making His power, as well as other tools, available for us to come out of any situation *VICTOROUSLY!*

One Bible verse that I have clung to over the past decade is, "Therefore, take up the full armor of God, so that you will be able to resist in the evil day, and having done everything, to stand firm" (Ephesian 6:13 NASB). A long time ago life's blows would send me crumbling to the ground. When the Lord began to train my hands for war and my fingers for battle (Psalm 144:1), life's blows would only make me lose my footing – I might stagger backwards a little bit. However, after even more maturing in the Lord, I realized the blows would only take my breath away for a moment. These days, the blows just lead me to bow my head in prayer. My prayer is for Him to be made strong in my weakness and to redeem the experience. He's a Redeemer!

If that's not victory I don't know what is, friends! People only associate victory with physical spoils and something tangible to show from the war. If I'm honest, so did I up until recently. But I'm learning that sometimes the most prized "possessions" from our victories are the things that can never be taken away from us. What the Lord did in my heart, mind, spirit, and soul in 2017 can never be taken away. EVER! For that I am thankful, ecstatic, and greatly humbled by His work in my life.

Romans 8:37 (NKJV) says, "Yet in all these things we are more than conquerors through Him who loved us." I am more than a conqueror. You are more than a conqueror. We, together, are more than conquerors. It does not matter what you are encountering in your life, there is a way for you to overcome and God has the winning strategy. Most of those strategies are contained in His love letter to us, the Bible. Again 2 Corinthians 4:8-10 says,

> We are pressed on every side by troubles, but we are not crushed. We are perplexed, but not driven to despair. We are hunted down, but never abandoned by God. We get knocked down, but we are not destroyed. Through suffering, our bodies continue to share in the death of Jesus so that the life of Jesus may also be seen in our bodies.

Get ready, my friends! We're going on a treasure hunt! The purpose of this hunt is to discover all the life hacks that will position us to slay every obstacle on our journey. I've already placed an order with the Treasury of Heaven. Our visual aids should be arriving here shortly. And I'm almost certain their delivery is much faster than Amazon Prime. I bet it gets here by the time you hit the next chapter. See you there!

know the truth about His character, who He is and what He's about, the better positioned we are to follow Him without question. When we understand that He is for us, that He died for us, and that He came into this world in order for us to have life more abundantly, we'll run in whatever direction He calls us *without question*! That's exactly how sheep stay safe, too. John 10:27 says, "My sheep listen to my voice; I know them, and they follow me." Even sheep know to follow their shepherd's voice and that's how they avert danger ... by listening and following closely.

On this journey with God, listening and sticking close to the shepherd is going to be key in our success. Here's what's cool about it all though: there is a bonus! All my action-adventure, cosplay, thespians peeps are about to get real hype! WE GET TO GET IN COSTUME!

In Chapter 1, I briefly spoke about the armor of God, and throughout this book I will be unpacking each piece in detail. We are given many tools in this Christian walk because Father God has set us up to be victorious. Yet it's up to us to *apply* the tools He's given us. An Amazon package sitting on your porch for days, weeks, or years simply isn't fulfilling its purpose. It's made it to its destination. And, yes, you have it in your possession. But if you don't unpack it and *use* what's been delivered to you, what's the point?

I think we all can agree, there is absolutely no point in having an umbrella in a downpour if you don't take the time to extend it, open it up, and position it over your head, correct? Not if you're trying to stay protected and dry anyway. Similarly, there are several different parts of the armor of God and we need to understand their purpose and how to apply them to our lives to be best protected. We've already established that we have an enemy and he wants to "steal, kill and destroy" us (John 10:10), so how can we position ourselves to be victorious?

Who doesn't get excited when an Amazon package shows up at their house? It never ceases to amaze me how pumped I get when my dishwasher detergent arrives. Or when my Garden of Life probiotics get here. Or even better when my favorite conditioner or hair products make it to me. I mean, does anyone else feel like it's Christmas when they see the smile on that Amazon Prime tape across that brown cardboard box. I often laugh at myself, because if I were to get those items under the Christmas tree as presents, I wouldn't be nearly as excited. But for whatever reason, receiving mundane items on my doorstep in everyday life *really* excites me. Hopefully it's not just me!

Imagine with me, you get saved (you make Jesus Lord of your life) and instantaneously a shipment arrives from the Throne Room of Heaven. You open it up and inside there's a card that says:

Welcome to the family!

Be strong in the Lord and in His mighty power. Enclosed you will find the full armor of God, so that you can take your stand against the devil's schemes. He's sneaky and will try to make you think you're fighting battles in the natural realm. For example, he'll plant thoughts in your mind and try to convince you that they are your thoughts. However, we're here to tell you, your upcoming struggles are not against flesh and blood, but against the rulers, against the authorities, against the powers of this dark world, and against the spiritual forces of evil in the heavenly realms ... basically demons. Yep, SURPRISE!

To maximize your win ratio, we suggest you put on the full armor of God, so that when the day of evil comes, you may be able to stand your ground, and after you have done everything, to stand ... STAND FIRM ... with the belt of truth buckled around your waist, with the breastplate of righteousness in place, and with your feet fitted with the readiness that comes from the gospel of peace. You're going to love these gospel shoes! But, THAT'S NOT ALL! In addition, take up the shield of faith, with which you can extinguish all the flaming arrows of the evil one. Take the helmet of salvation and the sword of the Spirit, which is the Word of God. BUT WAIT ... THERE'S MORE! Pray in the Spirit at all times and on every occasion. Yep, basically just stay in a place of prayer. You can make that happen anywhere at any point in your day. On this journey, staying alert and being persistent in your prayers is a must for all believers everywhere.

If you have any questions concerning the enclosed items, please refer to the operating manual, the Bible. Also 24/7 support is available through prayer, as mentioned above. And, another BONUS! When you have no idea what to pray, just pray in the Spirit and Holy Spirit will take over by inserting the most powerful prayers EVA! All of heaven is cheering for you! You've got this!

Now I imagine there are many different reactions you might have to this welcome message.

- Option 1: The warrior who was born ready. Think of any of the *300* movie gifs or memes. Like, you know, "I am Sparta!"
- Option 2: The fight or flight risk. Think of the meme with the little bucktooth blonde girl in her car seat giving us all the side eye. Fight/flight risks are undecided and could *book it* at any moment. However, they could also surprise you and be the most loyal!
- Option 3: The "peace out" reaction. Think of the Homer Simpson gif where he just starts slowly backing up and disappearing into the bushes. Deuces!

I'm sure there are many more reactions. However, those are the three I typically vacillate between when the Lord presents me with a new challenge. No matter how the welcome message makes you feel, I want to encourage you.

To my "I am Sparta" folks! Let's get it! You were made for this! God loves your boldness but don't get ahead of Him and His instructions. Obeying and following closely will be critical.

To my "fight or flight" folks! Congratulations! You are obviously taking time to count the cost. You won't be running headlong into anything unprepared and that will be an asset to you in war, my little strategists. At the end of the day, inquire of God how He wants you to proceed. Your peace will be found in obeying His instructions.

And lastly, for my "Homers," I want to encourage you with the words found in 2 Chronicles 20:15, "Listen, all you people … . This is what the LORD says: Do not be afraid! Don't be discouraged by this mighty army, for the battle is not yours, but God's." That means Papa God has your back! Not only that, He said the battle is His. It is our Commander in Chief leading us. He's taking it personally. He has a vested interest … and that's you!

So, let's unpack these goodies in the order they are packaged.

CHAPTER 4

Belt of Truth

*O*ne of my favorite fashion styles is a nice A-line dress accessorized with one of those wide-waist belts positioned at the natural waist. Luckily, it's one of those styles that keeps coming back. Not that I necessarily follow fashion trends. I tend to embrace my inner weirdo and do whatever I like. However, I love seeing that style! Depending on where I am in my fitness level, it's an effortless style: Dress, shoes, belt and I am out the door! But in "fluffier" seasons, I have to contend with one of the most insidious and evil tools the enemy can throw at a human being: back fat! Yup. Back fat.

Can we all just agree that back fat is from the devil and move on? K? K. So in "fluffier" seasons of life when I've tried to rock this style, I've had to constantly adjust said belt in the back because it's in a constant battle with the back fat. Insert the face palm emoji. But I'm here to encourage you! I believe God has designed your belt of truth FAR better than these wide-waist belts. It doesn't matter your body type in this scenario! Can I get an AMEN somebody!? So, let's jump into examining this shiny new belt freshly delivered from the Throne Room.

The Belt of Truth. The Matthew Henry Commentary says the belt "girds on [secures] all the other pieces of our armor." So basically, this belt of truth is going to be the piece that holds all the other pieces in place. How appropriate! I'm convinced that if we don't have a firm grip on the TRUTH of WHO God is and who WE are in Him, everything else falls apart.

First Peter 1:13 (NKJV) says this: "Therefore gird up the loins of your mind, be sober, and rest your hope fully upon the grace that is to be brought to you at the revelation of Jesus Christ."

The grace we receive for this fight comes straight from the revelation of who Jesus Christ is. Knowing Him. Trusting Him. Being confident He's for you and has your back. Girding our loins, securing the belt of truth around our waist, is what will give us the confidence to accomplish whatever God calls us to do. So, we're going to break up this truth, if you will, into two parts:

1. The truth of who God is.
2. The truth of who we are in Christ.

The Truth of Who God Is

So, what are the attributes of God? There are many and my intention is not to delve into all of them here. This is by no means a comprehensive list, however, I want to highlight a few of my favorites. The truth about God is …

God is **Good**. My friends, if you don't believe God is good, it's going to be a rough ride. You have to settle this matter in your heart and mind. Why would you follow and obey someone *willingly* if you don't believe they are a good person and have your best interest at heart? Psalm 34:8 (NASB) says, "O taste and see that the LORD is good; How blessed is the man who takes refuge in Him!" I encourage you to read all of Psalm 34. It's one of my favorites and I can't help but smile whenever I read it.

God is **Love**. I mean, one of the most obvious verses about His love for us and the extent He will go for that love is the most memorized verse ever! John 3:16 (NASB) says, "For God so loved the world, that He gave His only begotten Son, that whoever believes in Him shall not perish, but have eternal life." Can I throw an extra one in here for you … you know, because I'm such a giver. First John 4:8,16 tells us "But anyone who does not love does not know God, for God is love…. . We know how much God loves us, and we have put our trust in his love. God is love, and all who live in love live in God, and God lives in them."

God is **Gracious**. Like a good parent, He gives us grace. Let's face it. We're going to mess up. Sorry, not sorry, to all my perfectionists reading this. He gives us grace though. Read that last sentence again. Then read it three more times. This Christian walk is NOT on a tight rope thousands of feet in the air where one misstep sends you plunging to your death. It's just not!

Psalm 84:11 says, "For the Lord God is our sun and our shield. He gives us grace and glory. The Lord will withhold no good thing from those who do what is right." If the posture of our heart is to do right, He honors that. And guess what? Even when the posture of our heart is to *flat out sin*, He gives us grace when we choose to repent. Repent means we turn in a different direction and posture our hearts to do what's right. Repentance is key. This isn't a sloppy grace that allows us to keep sinning and in essence destroy our lives in the process. It's a grace that helps us to course correct and get back on track. Remember I said He's a *good* parent.

Romans 5:15 says, "But there is a great difference between Adam's sin and God's gracious gift. For the sin of this one man, Adam, brought death to many. But even greater is God's wonderful grace and his gift of forgiveness to many through this other man, Jesus Christ."

God is **Holy**. Do you realize that all the angels and creatures in heaven *literally* sing day and night, "Holy, holy, holy, is the Lord God almighty" (Revelations 4:8b). Nonstop. Every. Single. Day. God's holiness is serious business.

First Samuel 2:2 says, "No one is holy like the Lord! There is no one besides you; there is no Rock like our God." And guess what? His desire is for us to be holy as well.

First Peter 1:15-16 tells us, "But now you must be holy in everything you do, just as God who chose you is holy. For the Scriptures say, 'You must be holy because I am holy.'" Before you stress out, He gives us the strength to do what He's called us to do.

Two of my all-time *favorite* worship songs are "Lord You're Holy" by Eddie James and "Holy" by Matt Gilman. I encourage you to pause right here,

Google them and just listen to them both. Just close your eyes, bask in the words, and soak them up. This is the God you serve. You'll thank me later.

God is **Omnipotent**. He literally has unlimited power and there is NOTHING He cannot do. You do not serve a lame God. Never forget that. It doesn't matter what the situation looks like, He's undefeated.

Job 42:1-2 says, "Then Job answered the Lord and said, 'I know that You can do all things, and that no purpose of Yours can be thwarted.'"

And one of my favorites, Luke 1:37, says "For nothing will be impossible with God."

Also, I love those verses where we see God flexin'. Haha! You know, those verses like Jeremiah 32:27 that says, "Behold, I am the Lord, the God of all flesh; is anything too difficult for Me?"

Let 'em know, God. Let 'em know!

God is **Omnipresent**. This means He is present everywhere at the same time.

Proverbs 15:3 says, "The eyes of the Lord are in every place, watching the evil and the good."

And Psalm 139:5 reminds us that, "You have enclosed me behind and before, and laid Your hand upon me."

You are never alone, my friend. He is always with you. Whether you feel His presence or not, trust that He is literally right there with you.

God is **Righteous**. He is morally right, justifiable, virtuous. God always does what is right. It's been said that righteousness is holiness in action. I love that! So, because His nature is Holy, it leads Him to do what is right. Isaiah 45:21 says,

> Consult together, argue your case.
> Get together and decide what to say.
> Who made these things known so long ago?
> What idol ever told you they would happen?
> Was it not I, the Lord?
> For there is no other God but me,
> a righteous God and Savior.
> There is none but me.

Boom!

God is **Sovereign**. He is the supreme or ultimate power. One of my favorite verses on His sovereignty is Romans 8:28 which says, "And we know that God causes everything to work together for the good of those who love God and are called according to his purpose for them."

And Colossian 1:16-17 says,

> ... or through him God created everything
> in the heavenly realms and on earth.
> He made the things we can see
> and the things we can't see—
> such as thrones, kingdoms, rulers, and authorities in the unseen world.
> Everything was created through him and for him.
> He existed before anything else,
> and he holds all creation together.

He knows the number of hairs on your head! When I think of His sovereignty, I think of the children's song titled "He's Got the Whole World in His Hands." That was my jam as a kid!

We could do this all day ... really. If you want to deeply expound on His attributes further, I highly recommend a book by A.W. Tozer titled *The Attributes of God*. Dive deep. Secure His identify in your mind and heart because it's the only way you'll become settled in your own identity in Christ as well. Trust me. I've watched people get taken out left and right because they were not convinced of the truth of God's identity and their identity in Him. It's foundational.

Now let's pause for a moment of reflection.

First off, I want to say if you struggled with any of these attributes of God that I just listed, that's great news! You may ask, "Say what now?" There is absolutely no condemnation and there is no shame there. If something didn't sit right with you, take it as an open invitation from God to further unpack it. There's also no purpose in trying to hide the fact that you may be unsettled or to try to fake it until you make it. Why? Because God already knows all of your inner thoughts. Ready for a bonus attribute?

God is **Omniscient**. That means He's all-knowing.

Psalm 139:4 says, "Even before there is a word on my tongue, Behold, O Lord, You know it all."

And Psalm 44:21 reminds us, "Would not God find this out? For He knows the secrets of the heart."

If He's highlighting an attribute, or if it's making you uncomfortable, that is an *invitation* to dive deeper! There's possibly a crack in your foundation and now is the time to examine it and repair it. This is exciting news! It's like the old saying goes, "The first step is admitting there's a problem." Problems that are identified and highlighted are in the best position to be addressed and corrected, right!? Be encouraged! He wants to partner with you to seal up the crack and secure you further in your walk with Him!

The Truth of Who We Are in Christ

So, let's get this out of the way right off the bat: You are NOT the sum of the things that have happened to you in life. Your identity is also NOT the things you may have done in your past. That is not *who* you *are*! Being rejected by those who should have supported you does not make you a reject! Having lived through being molested or sexually assaulted does not mean you are damaged goods or something to be used by others! Your parents putting you up for adoption does not mean you are unwanted and unworthy of being loved. If you had an abortion in your past, it doesn't mean that you're a murderer for life with no hope of being redeemed. Just because you lived a promiscuous life for a season doesn't ruin your future or your destiny forever. I could go on and on and on.

None of these things disqualifies you. None of these things changes God's view of you either. There is always hope. There is always redemption being offered at the table. There is no such thing as too far gone in the kingdom of God! One of His names is Kinsman Redeemer! Take that, devil!

Let me share with you a quick story. Recently, on a Sunday morning before church, Lord impressed someone on my heart to pray for. As I was praying for them, He kept showing me the word, "reconcile." In the context of what He had me praying, it wasn't making sense to me. I prayed and asked God for more revelation. A few hours later at church my pastor was preaching and digressed for a moment to give us the definition of the word "reconciliation." I immediately perked up because I knew God was going to give me some insight on my prayer time earlier.

My pastor goes on to say, "reconciliation is restoring something back to its original design or function." Hmmmmm, the pieces were falling into place. I realized that God was telling me it was His will to reconcile this person back to their original calling, identity, and destiny. It was a beautiful revelation!

I was serving on the worship team that day and when we were singing the closing song He gave me even more revelation. The closing song was "Better Word" by Leeland. The entire song is about the power of the blood of Jesus and how it speaks a "better word" over our lives. His blood is what we look to to measure our worth. It was shed for us. That's how precious you are to God!

The part of the song that wrecked me that morning was the part that explains how the blood is essentially revising our history and how it covers us with the calling God sent us down to earth with. Wow guys! I was completely undone! God was basically telling me to pray that the blood of Jesus would reconcile this person back to their original purpose and destiny. He wanted me to agree with His Spirit that the blood of Jesus would redeem this person's past and give them a clean slate and new passion to pursue their destiny. I could barely sing I was so choked up! That's how Papa feels about you! That's who we are in Christ.

Earlier I exposed some common lies that the enemy uses to ambush our destiny. Now I'm going to take some time to share where our real identity comes from. There is a beautiful passage in scripture that gives us a glimpse into how purposeful God was when it came to creating each one of us individually. Psalm 139:14-18 goes like this:

> Thank you for making me so wonderfully complex!
> Your workmanship is marvelous—how well I know it.
> You watched me as I was being formed in utter seclusion,
> as I was woven together in the dark of the womb.
> You saw me before I was born.
> Every day of my life was recorded in your book.
> Every moment was laid out
> before a single day had passed.

How precious are your thoughts about me, O God.
They cannot be numbered!
I can't even count them; they outnumber the grains of sand!
And when I wake up,
you are still with me!

That scripture gives me all the fan-girling vibes, let me tell ya! God is the lover of our souls! I try to imagine God's face as He created me, and as He specifically created you. Don't picture an assembly line! This was a not a copy/paste job! Picture a potter's wheel and you're the clay. He's forming you personally, intimately, very intentionally. This is customization as its best! There are so many great scriptures in the Bible with the Potter/clay analogy:

Isaiah 64:8 says, "And yet, O Lord, you are our Father. We are the clay, and you are the potter. We all are formed by your hand."

Formed by His hands. Not an impersonal pottery machine; *His hands*. We are handmade and handcrafted. I wish I had really gotten that revelation and meditated on this truth when I was growing up. It would have been so helpful for me. There were many times I didn't really like myself because I wasn't like the others around me. You may struggle with that as well. It may be mostly because you're taking on the expectations others are projecting upon you. No matter the reason, we *must* gird ourselves in truth, God's truth. Not the opinions of others, not even our own opinions of ourselves!

What God says about us is the baseline and everything that contradicts that needs to be thrown out. Isaiah 29:16 says,

How foolish can you be? He is the Potter, and he is certainly greater than you, the clay! Should the created thing say of the one who made it, "He didn't make me"? Does a jar ever say, "The potter who made me is stupid"?

LOL! I laugh, but how many times have we questioned how God made us? He doesn't make mistakes. He never has and He never will.

When a potter is creating a vessel, he doesn't sit down and say, "Whelp, let's see what comes out of this lump of nothing." He sits down with a vision in mind. "I'm going to make a bowl today." Or, "Today I want make a very special cup specifically designed for taking communion."

My friend, *YOU* were designed by God for a very specific purpose. You were sent into this world at a strategically appointed time/season in the earth to accomplish said purpose. He *sees* you. He *loves* you. He wants to *partner* with you on your mission, really and truly! Stop looking to the right and to the left to see what others are doing. While we will encounter people in life who have similar purposes, interests, passions, and desires, there is only one YOU! My point is, if you haven't figured it out yet, your identity is unique to you! Be unapologetically YOU!

This is one of the main things the enemy attacks: our purpose and identity. He tries to force our hand into trying to find purpose and identity in everything other than our Creator. Movies, television, social media, political agendas, music, friends, significant others, culture, even church leaders. We are constantly being inundated with voices trying to convince us of who we are or who we should be. Voices telling us what we should think, what we should be doing, and how we should look.

So, let me ask you a question. When you buy that new air fryer, lawn mower, or cell phone, where is your first stop when trying to find out how to use it? I hope you thought, "The maker of the product via the user manual." You see where I'm going here? Yup. Maker = God. Manual = Bible.

Get rooted and grounded in who He designed you to be by talking to Him and spending time with Him. One of the best ways to do that is to get as much truth (the Word of God) in you as possible. This gives you the power and authority to throw the lies away! Many of you have probably heard about the way people are trained to spot counterfeit money. Surprise, surprise! The strategy is not by studying what fake money looks like. Instead, it's by studying *real* currency. Becoming an expert on what real money looks like. Once you are extremely acquainted with the *real* thing, it's easier to spot the fake ones. Let me give you an example of what that looks like.

One of the ways the enemy tries to weaken us in this battle is by infiltrating our thoughts. These thoughts will sound like your own thoughts, but they're not. He's a liar and very cunning. Keep in mind that the fruits of the spirit are love, joy, peace, patience, kindness, goodness, faithfulness, gentleness, and self-control (Galatian 5:22-23). If the thoughts you have do not make you feel these things, they are more than likely not from God. Once you become seriously acquainted with TRUTH, it's easier to spot the lies.

I invite you to do a prophetic act with me. Pull out a piece of paper and make a list of all the nonsense the enemy has harassed you with for years:

> You're not good enough to …
> It's too late for you to …
> You're a reject.
> You're not loveable.
> You're too undesirable.
> No one likes you.
> You're too much.
> You'll never make it.

Now sometimes he gets us to believe and agree with these lies, so we need to break those agreements. It's very simple, actually. I was talking to a friend recently, and she got really overwhelmed by a project she felt God called her to do. In the course of our conversation she said, "I'm just not cut out for *xyz*." Now there was a process that resulted in those words coming out of her mouth. First, the enemy planted the thought. He doesn't want her stepping into her destiny, so he plants lies. Secondly, she got duped into accepting the thought as her own. Meaning she didn't recognize it was an intruder. Thirdly, she heard the lie enough that she actually started to *agree* with it and believe it was true. Fourthly, she confessed it out loud with her own mouth.

I stopped her right there. I pointed out what I was observing:

"God gave you a mission. You hit some roadblocks attempting to complete said mission. The enemy hit you with a lie. You agreed with him in your mind. Now you're confessing it with your own mouth. That's his strategy – to shut you down with of the power of your words and confession. Now it's time to repent, change your confession, and get back on track."

I heard radio silence followed by, "Wooooow girl!" Right! He gets the best of us with this played-out tactic. But now we're hip to his game.

CHAPTER 5
Putting on the Belt of Truth

Stand your ground, putting on the belt of truth ... .
Ephesians 6:14

I felt very unseen and unheard while I was growing up. You can chalk it up to middle child syndrome, but I believe it was much deeper than that. As a child, I used to watch a TV show called Sesame Street. There was a song they used to sing that I related to all too well (and for what seemed like the wrong reasons). The song was called "One of These Things." The objective of the song and activity was to show kids four different items in a grid. One of them was obviously very different from the other three. After the song was played, the kids would have an opportunity to point out the one thing that was different from the other three. Sometimes it would be three circles and one square. Or three yellow objects and one red. You get the point.

In my family, I was definitely the "different" item. Surrounded by mostly introverts, I was the one extreme extrovert. Surrounded by homebodies, I was the one who wanted to go out with friends and do all the extracurricular activities. I was made to feel like my personality wasn't acceptable. If I had a dollar for every time I was asked, "Why can't you just stay home?" Or

"Why do you have to sign up for that club too?" or "What is so great about being outside?" I'd be retired by now. I honestly didn't have an answer to any of those questions. It's just what I gravitated toward. It's what brought me joy and made me happy. I didn't have the language for it then, but it's what filled my love tank. Now I know the very definition of an extrovert is someone who is recharged by social activities and the company of people.

For years, I honestly felt like something was wrong with me. To add insult to injury, I was also very outspoken, blunt, and to the point. Being raised in a Haitian family where children were pretty much to be seen and not heard, it was truly a recipe for disaster. I adopted the unhealthy habit of minimizing who I was around my family pretty early on. My friends at school got the full version of my personality in living color, but once I got home I spent most of the time just trying to fit in … and failing miserably.

I was raised in a church where people seemed more concerned with how you dressed, your behavior, and reputation than your character and your heart. It was all about outward appearances. I felt like church was more about not wearing pants, not wearing jewelry, and not wearing skirts that were too short than it was about Jesus.

My family was in church whenever the doors were opened, or at least it seemed that way. I was a Christian … or so I thought. My dad was a deacon and preached every now and then and my mom was very involved with the women's ministry and taught Sunday school. Things were great … well more like palatable. What could possibly go wrong!?

In November of 1995, my mom announced we were moving from Philadelphia to Atlanta. She was a nurse and had accepted a new opportunity.

I. WAS. LIVID!

I was wrapping up the first semester of my junior year in high school. I'd been attending school with the same friends since the third grade. Were my parents seriously uprooting me a year and a half before graduating high school with my crew? Unbelievable! No amount of begging to stay with friends to finish out high school in Pennsylvania was successful.

So, in December of 1995, a few days after my 16th birthday, we moved to Atlanta. Let the games begin, right!? When I arrived at my new school, I was the new girl with the chip on her shoulder. I was not at all happy to be there and I had no intention of trying to pretend with these people. I'm not gonna lie, it was a brutal transition for me. Looking back on all that, I know God kept me because I could have fallen into all kinds of trouble. I could have gone down many different "wrong" roads ... but God!

In the spring of 1996, a new friend of mine from school invited me to a youth event her church was putting on called Disciple Now. It was a weekend retreat where we'd spend a weekend with a host family to fellowship and draw closer to God. By some kind of miracle, the parents who raised me for 16 years and *never* allowed me to go on a sleepover APPROVED for me to sleep over at some stranger's house for an ENTIRE WEEKEND! I was stunned! I was obviously being set up by God. However, at the time, I was convinced Jesus was coming back that very day because this was end-of-the-world type of behavior from my parents!

I got to the retreat, met some new people, and played a lot of games, like basketball. That's the weekend I got my nickname Ca-Shaq, LOL! For some reason, I was endued with the power to play great basketball that weekend. The anointing left the second the weekend was over, so don't get too excited. He gives and takes away, I guess. Haha!

The last night of the retreat, our leaders challenged us to take some time to find a quiet corner of the house and get alone with God to see what was on His heart. Now up until this point in my life, I honestly considered myself a Christian. I mean, I was at church every single time the doors were open. Back in Philly, I was part of the youth choir. My dad was a deacon. Did I mention that, after we moved to Atlanta, my father accepted an offer to become the Senior Pastor of a local church? So now I was officially a PK (Pastor's Kid). What that has to do with anything I don't know, but these were the facts.

When I sat down with God that last night of the retreat, I wasn't really sure what would happen or what to expect. I chose to just sit there in silence until I got an impression. And then I heard Him. It wasn't an audible voice or anything. However, it was a strong sense of hearing Him in my mind. I clearly heard him say to me, "You do know that you're not getting to heaven on your preacher daddy's coattails, right?"

SAY WHAAAAAAAAAAT!? Insert the "mindblown" emoji!

Was God actually implying that I was not saved? Hmph! I sat there for the longest moment, stunned. Not only was this the clearest I had ever heard God speak to me in my entire life, but what He had just told me rocked me to the core! But there wasn't one ounce of condemnation in His tone. Not in the least. There was nothing but love and a desire to guide me to where I needed to be. He was simply alerting me that there was a disconnect and a *major* crack in my foundation. Or better yet, there was no foundation at all! He was helping me connect the dots. After a moment, I literally laughed out loud while tears streamed down my face. My first real encounter with the Creator God, and come to find out this Dude was funny! Yes capitol "D" Dude. This is God we're talking about after all. Let's not be disrespectful!

That was the beginning of the end for me. The end of that stale "Christianity" I'd been living. The end of the impersonal religion I'd been partaking in. I felt the warmth of His love in that one-liner and that changed the trajectory of my entire life. Real Christianity was about a *relationship* with **Jesus**! A Christian literally means a follower of Christ. Do you follow people you don't know or have no relationship with? I hope not. That could land you in all kinds of hot water and come with all kinds of strong, judge-y labels like "stalker." Just sayin'.

Back in the day, I knew people who used to get super offended by the "Jesus is my Homeboy" t-shirts. Do they still make those? I need one. I don't remember their origin, but I remember those shirts made me smile whenever I saw them. They reminded me of a scripture that talks about Jesus being a "friend that sticks closer than a brother." It's about a relationship.

Once I got to know who He was, that's when God started explaining to me just how much He loved Cassandra! Me! And not only did He love me, He specifically designed me and sent me into this world ... get this ... FOR A PURPOSE! I felt seen for the first time in my life. If I'm completely candid, I had one person in my life – a grade school friend – who I felt really saw me and loved me just the way I was. To everyone else in my life, I felt like you could remove me (cut) and replace me (paste) with another black girl with the same height and build and no one would even notice I was missing. That's not how it is with God the Father.

It's easy to recite, "For God so loved the world that He gave His only begotten son. That whosoever believes in Him shall not perish but have ever lasting life" (John 3:16 NKJV) without a single ounce of emotion. But there comes a moment in your walk with Christ where it feels so real and so personal that you can replace "the world" and "whosoever" with your own name. You become completely undone by His abundant love for YOU! He sees you! That's what that Disciple Now weekend did for me. It started me on a journey to get my Belt of Truth. I started learning the truth of who God is: His character, nature, and attributes. It also started me on my journey to knowing my identity in Christ: How He created me and who He created me to be. He also began showing me what my purpose on this earth was. I went from feeling bad for always wanting to "hang out" with people to Him telling me He's called me to be an influencer. I was someone called to mentor, assist, and champion people. How else would I do that if I'm not around people on a regular basis, forming meaningful relationships?

I tend to be a loud talker. I've been working on it my entire life. I went from being embarrassed because I was so loud to Him explaining to me that He gave me a loud voice because He intended to use me as His mouthpiece. I'm called to prophesy and speak domestically and internationally. I went from feeling bad because I was always being told I was bossy. Now I understand that He had placed a leadership calling and anointing on my life. I went from feeling bad about being so blunt and stern to realizing I had a prophetic call on my life. He was calling me to be unwavering concerning His truths. He was making it clear that He was calling me to be *me* … and I was eating it all up!

These were all gifts that He had placed in me on purpose. Did I need to hone those gifts and skills a bit? Absolutely! Did I have some fine-tuning that needed to be done in my life? Definitely! I still do. However, knowing that I was not a reject in God's eyes was a game changer for me. There are no words to explain the impact of going through life feeling defective and broken and then all of a sudden understanding that you are just exactly the way God designed and created you to be! That's part of being girded in truth, too.

First Thessalonian 5:21 says, "As you begin your journey to gird your-self in truth, I encourage you to test all things; hold fast what is good." I also encourage you to "not be conformed to this world, but be transformed by the renewing of your mind, that you may prove what is that good and acceptable and perfect will of God" (Romans 12:2 NKJV).

Be unapologetically you! God is the expert when it comes to who you are and your identity. He is your source and has your owner's manual. He's your Creator and you are not defective. You will encounter many people and things in life that will try to rewire you and repurpose you. Do not allow it! Go back to the source! Solidify your foundation of who He is and who He created you to be. You'll never be at peace until you do.

Genesis 1:31 says, "God saw all that he had made, and it was very good." He created you and said it was good! He wants you to see yourself the same way. Go forth and be great!

CHAPTER 6

Breastplate of Righteousness

I remember going out with some coworkers for lunch one day several years ago. At the end of the meal, as everyone was settling their tabs, I discovered an error on mine. As some people were standing and getting ready to leave, a few of them asked me what the hold-up was. I told them that I noticed that my bill was wrong. I had ordered three side items as my meal and was only charged for two of them. They all looked at me like I had grown a second head. I knew what they were thinking, but my conscience would not allow me to leave without bringing it to the server's attention. Best case scenario, she would say, "Oh, thank you for being honest" and let me have the third side item for free. In this case, she thanked me for my honesty, corrected my bill, I paid for all three items and left in peace. You can't put a price on the peace that comes from doing the right thing. You also can't put a price on character.

God sees everything. I believe that when we're faithful in the little things, He can trust us with the bigger things, and so He blesses us with more. Remember the Parable of the Talents in Matthew 25:14–30? Three servants were given stewardship over money. One was lazy and shady, one put in minimal effort, and the last one did his best. When the boss man came back and assessed what each worker had done, he chastised the lazy worker. He even took what he originally gave the lazy worker and gave it to the one who did his best so he could steward it. Righteousness comes at a price. In my example above, at the restaurant, it *literally* cost me. I believe that when we participate in many actions that lack integrity, it begins to erode away at our conscience and our heart. On top of that, we reap what sow.

I remember hearing a preacher explain that when someone has an affair they didn't just make one poor choice. Affairs rarely go from eyes meeting to immediately jumping in bed with someone. Affairs are usually a series of poor choices, ignoring warnings, and a lack of conviction that eventually culminate in the final act. Now there's something to ponder as we dive into righteousness.

So let's go back to our Throne Room "Amazon" box and unpack the next item. Oooooh ... shiny! The Breastplate of Righteousness! So what do we do with this thing? What's its purpose? The breastplate on the Roman soldier's armor was often made out of chains and was designed to protect the soldier's vital organs, like his heart. Paul calls it, in the Ephesians analogy, the Breastplate of Righteousness. Righteousness means the quality of being morally right or justifiable. Doing what is right and good.

Did you know your morals, thoughts, and purity of heart affect your battle against the enemy? This is not about legalism. But at the same time, Proverbs 4:23 tells us, "Keep your heart with all diligence, for out of it *springs* the issues of life." Other versions say, "Guard your heart ... ."

We've all heard the phrase "trash in, trash out" concerning various areas of our lives, but it also applies to our spiritual lives. As someone who has come out of a legalistic background, I'm not even about to tell you what you should and shouldn't do on the gray area items (although the Bible is explicitly clear on many issues). Everyone handles different situations in different ways. However, we really need to be aware of and know how to assess our personal weaknesses in order to apply wisdom to protect any cracks in our armor.

What may be acceptable for one person may be not beneficial for you. First Corinthians 10:23 (CSB) says, "'Everything is permissible,' but not everything is helpful. 'Everything is permissible,' but not everything builds up." GOD's WORD Translation (GW) says it this way, "Someone may say, 'I'm allowed to do anything,' but not everything is helpful. I'm allowed to do anything, but not everything encourages growth."

I'll share a personal example. When I got saved, the concept of tithing was not foreign to me. Having grown up in a Christian home with parents who were faithful givers, it had been modeled in front of me. The only real question for me surfaced in my 20s when I found myself around people who were debating whether we should tithe off of the gross amount or net amount of our paychecks. Anyone who knows me knows I'm not a debater. I love a good discussion. However, I don't debate and argue for fun. I also don't touch explosive topics around people who don't know how to have those conversations while still honoring the people they're speaking to. So, I honestly didn't participate in the discussion as it was getting heated. However, it did get me thinking.

Don't you find it interesting that there are many warnings not to test God in the Word? However, tithing/giving is the one area where God actually invites us to test Him. Malachi 3:10 says:

> Bring the whole tithe into the storehouse, that there may be food in my house. Test me in this," says the LORD Almighty, "and see if I will not throw open the floodgates of heaven and pour out so much blessing that there will not be room enough to store it.

God made it very clear to me early in my walk that one of my gifts/callings was giving. All believers are called to tithe. However, I knew that I was someone who was called to give lavishly and I truly enjoy it. Concerning the Gross vs. Net debate, my mindset was this … I could go searching out the scriptures, do a scholarly key word search, and study Hebrew and Greek for a week. But naw … I'm good. I just made an executive decision that night. I still wasn't sure which was right, but I knew if I decided to tithe off the gross I'd be covered either way. That was my deep philosophical decision-making process. And then I moved on with my life. Haha! So, I was a faithful gross tither from that point on. But don't be too impressed yet. I definitely don't mind sharing my epic fails with you, too! It's all about transparency.

Once upon a time, when I was a teenager, I had an intense moment where I honestly battled being obedient to tithe. In this instance, it was because there was something I really wanted to buy and I let greed get the best of me. So that Sunday, I did not put my tithes in the offering basket and I left church and headed straight to the mall ... like Sméagol coming for his *Precious*. In the process, I made a poor judgment call and ran a red light by mistake. I was immediately pulled over by a cop and given a ticket. I kid you not, the amount of the ticket was the *exact* amount of the tithe that I skipped out on that Sunday. Yeah, that one stung a little.

The Lord taught me a very valuable lesson with that. Some might say the speeding ticket had nothing to do with the disobedience to tithe. However, I knew in my heart God was getting my attention. That night He spoke to my heart very simply. "Would you rather give that money to the church and be a part of advancing the kingdom and be blessed in return? Or would you rather give that money to the County Police Department, Cassandra?" Lesson learned. Case closed. I never missed a tithe payment again, LOL! Willful disobedience will remove God's hand of protection over certain areas of your life and the enemy is just waiting for a way in.

First Peter 5:8 says, "Stay alert! Watch out for your great enemy, the devil. He prowls around like a roaring lion, looking for someone to devour." Ummmm ... no. I am not the one! I'll take a heaping serving of obedience, please and thank you!

So, like I said, the enemy is looking for cracks in your armor, your breastplate. And guess what? When he finds sin, he has a legal right to harass and torment you. Sin will open the door wide to his antics and your lack of conviction is the welcome mat. There are many different ways the enemy can enter in legally. While I won't be diving deep into each one, please consider whether there is an area you need to repent of and seal up. Here are a few to get you started:

Unforgiveness – the poison you drink hoping it affects the other person
Occultic practices – horoscopes, ouji boards, witchcraft, hypnotism
Soul Ties – sex partners outside of marriage
Lying – Remember satan's nickname? Yeah ... the Father of Lies
Stealing – anything you take in a dishonest fashion

The list can go on and on. However, God is faithful to show us which areas we need to focus on in any given season. Matter of fact, let's do an activation right now! I mean why not? We're already here! I invite you to pray this prayer with me:

> Holy Spirit I invite You to come. Thank You that You champion me in all things. Thank You for being the faithful Helper in my life. Holy Spirit, would you come and show me if there is an area in my life where I've left the door open to the enemy?

Just listen. What was the first thought, picture, or impression you got? Grab the very first thought. If He showed you something (whether it's from the list above or something completely different), pray this prayer with me:

> Thank You, Holy Spirit, that You are for me! Thank You for exposing the scheme of the enemy in my life. No weapon formed against me will prosper. So today I repent for _____.
> There is no temptation that has overtaken me but that which is common to man. I lay down _____ and I commit to following in Your ways. Thank You, God, for setting me free! In Jesus' name I pray. Amen!

He is a good shepherd and He will complete the good work He has begun in us. I love how 1 Corinthians 10:13 and Isaiah 54:17 help us in this area.

> The temptations in your life are no different from what others experience. And God is faithful. He will not allow the temptation to be more than you can stand. When you are tempted, he will show you a way out so that you can endure. (1 Corinthians 10:13)

> "No weapon formed against you shall prosper, And every tongue *which* rises against you in judgment You shall condemn. This *is* the heritage of the servants of the LORD, And their righteousness *is* from Me," Says the LORD. (Isaiah 54:17 NKJV)

Be encouraged! Righteousness is our heritage! Wear that breastplate of righteousness with pride! Putting it on is simply our commitment to aligning with God's ways and making a choice to walk uprightly. Be the proud son and daughter of the Most High King! Never forget who you are and *whose* you are.

CHAPTER 7

Putting on the Breastplate
of Righteousness

Stand your ground, putting on... the body armor of God's righteousness.
Ephesians 6:14

A very foundational aspect of righteousness is integrity. Integrity is defined in the Oxford Dictionary as "the quality of being honest and having strong moral principles; moral uprightness."

One of my all-time favorite quotes is by John Wooden. He said, "Be more concerned with your character than your reputation, because your character is what you really are, while your reputation is merely what others think you are." That quote was a light in a very dark place for me for many, many years.

There was a season of my life where I felt like certain people who lacked character seemed to be getting away with it, scot-free. While I felt like I was doing my best to walk in integrity, I continued to shoulder the consequences of their actions. Three things the Lord kept reminding of during that trying season was the Wooden quote above and the two verses coming up.

Galatians 6:9, "So let's not get tired of doing what is good. At just the right time we will reap a harvest of blessing if we don't give up."

And Psalms 126:5, "Those who plant in tears will harvest with shouts of joy."

And let me testify of the other side of that trial. I am reaping a harvest of blessing that I could not even conceive! One of the main things I hear from people these days when they see me is, "Wow! You look so happy!" or "You look so much younger, what is going on with you?" or "The Joy of the Lord is all over you." Haha! I usually smile and say thank you because it sounds way better than … "I was finally delivered from the most intense battle of my life and it just feels good to be alive and free from the grip of my enemy!" Yeah, see my point? Sometimes it's better to just smile and nod.

Having integrity and living righteously is all about being conformed to the likeness of Christ. It's not strictly about behavior modification. Although, some people (especially new believers) probably see spiritual disciplines as behavior modification, the end game is to get our heart in sync with His. Here's another way to look at it …

There are many ways to lose weight. There are a ton of fad diets, pills, etc. Sure, they may work for a limited time, however, the most ideal change would be a lifestyle change, correct? Re-think what you're eating. What are the best foods for *your* body. Rethink your activity level? Find an activity you actually love. Invest in it and commit to making it part of your lifestyle.

Coming back to the spiritual application, righteousness is an inside job. It starts in your heart and it's a life-long change we're making. The enemy will use many outside resources, any willing vessel, to completely shatter that seed of righteousness you're trying to cultivate.

If you've ever heard of Graham Cooke and follow his ministry, you're familiar with his term "grace growers." When I heard him speak at a local church several years ago, his revelation on the term really rocked me. In a Facebook post back in 2012 he said it this way, "Nasty people are our grace growers. They provide us (unconsciously!) a shortcut into the nature of God's kindness, love, and goodness. Learn to spot the opportunity in the crisis and take advantage!"

Wheeeeeewwww LAWD! Let me get real for a minute. I'm from Philly. You see where I'm going with this? I was not raised in the sweat tea drinking, "bless your heart" South. I was raised in Philly where people are straight shooters. They don't ask, "How are you?" unless they really care, and they're considered blunt to the point of "rudeness." Yes, rudeness is in quotes because everyone's definition of rude is not the same.

I was not raised in an environment where people sugarcoated things. I have absolutely zero issues confronting anybody, about anything, at any time. The only times in my life I can remember not confronting someone about a problem and expressing how I really felt was when the Holy Spirit would check me with a "nope," "not now," or "rephrase/reword that please." Ha! Let's just say one of the verses the Holy Spirit would remind me of consistently was Philippians 4:8 which says, "Let your gentleness be known to all men. The Lord *is at hand.*"

In the beginning my response would always be, "Who? Me? Gentle? Bahahahahahahahah!" I've come a long way guys, trust and believe. Although the Holy Spirit was doing this gentle work in my life, I've encountered many tests along the way. Years ago, I worked a job with a supervisor who had a personal vendetta against me. It's one of the most bizarre situations I have lived through to date.

When I was hired for this job, things seemed pretty normal. My new boss showed me the cubical that was assigned to me and over the course of the week I began to make it my own. I put up some family pictures, some small posters with scriptures, and other silly things. One of my favorite posters was one where the top half showed a blue frown face with the words "My life before Jesus" above it. The bottom half had a psychedelic feel with flowers and a yellow smiley face that read "My life after Jesus." One day, about a week into my new job, my boss came over to my desk to tell me something. I noticed she stopped mid-sentence when her eyes fell on the Bible sitting on my desk. It wasn't open so she had to know I wasn't sitting there reading it on the clock. It always sat there. I would usually read it on my 15-minute breaks and sometimes during my lunch breaks. She was obviously not excited about it sitting there. As a matter of fact, whenever she'd come to my desk, her eyes would always go to my Bible and she'd get a disapproving look on her face.

I couldn't tell if this was her way of making a passive aggressive statement or what. Either way, I wasn't fazed. I had already made up my mind that the Bible wasn't going anywhere, period! After weeks of her behaving that way, and me making no changes to my setup, her animosity toward me just grew. That usually happens when people start getting the memo that you won't easily be bullied. Meanwhile, I would simply smile and treat her with respect. Even my other teammates would comment on how baffled they were with her treatment of me. They may not have known what was going on, but I did. I was in the middle of some spiritual warfare.

To make matters worse … for Hell … I decided to host a weekly Bible study. I mean, I was already in the doghouse, why not go for broke, right? I had selected a Kay Arthur Precept study. Some coworkers and I set out on this Bible study adventure during our lunch breaks once a week. This seemed to aggravate my boss even further. She would start making passive aggressive comments about being sure we were back from lunch on time. The Lord had warned me from the onset to operate this study with excellence and integrity and I even shared that with the other attendees. He stressed we needed to honor our leaders and to make sure to come back on time. So nice try, devil, but Holy Spirit was already a step ahead of you.

As a matter fact, that was the main reason I chose the Kay Arthur study to begin with. It was a 40-minute study. I knew this would give folks time to wrap up any conference calls that were running over. We'd start at 12:10 and end at 12:50 on the dot every time. I wasn't going to give the enemy *any* ammo against me and the coworkers joining me. I felt very protective of my peers and didn't want them to start receiving the same treatment I was getting from my boss.

So, when she couldn't find fault in what we were doing from an HR perspective, or with the quality of my work, a new strategy was launched against us. All of a sudden, the conference room that we had been meeting in for weeks was booked out from under us. This new "meeting" was now at the *same time* on the *same days* for the next several months. What a *co-inky dink*! You could argue, "Well, Cassandra, it *is* a place of business. Work meetings have to be prioritized over extracurricular Bible studies." To that point I would agree. However, what was happening was that the room would be booked but *no one* would ever be *in there* actually using it. I saw a meeting happen maybe once or twice, but it certainly was not consistent.

I was not a happy camper! I began venting to the Lord, asking Him how He could let this happen. We were making such great progress in the study. Folks were surrendering their lives to Christ. People were repenting of sin. People were recommitting to reading the Word daily on their own. Folks were asking for prayer about serious matters they were dealing with in life. This blow with the conference room just seemed to come at the worst time. BUT GOD! These grace growers were about to learn a lesson.

One afternoon I was called to meet with some other departmental leaders on the other end of the building. While heading there, I noticed a room door that was ajar. It looked like a conference room, but not one I'd never seen or been in before. I peeked in and was surprised to find a smaller conference room, with a conference table, surrounded by tons of boxes. I immediately knew this was the Lord's strategy for me to get my Bible study back on track. I contacted HR and asked them if I could use the room and I got a green light. That day on my lunch break, I moved boxes! I pushed them all as far back and piled them as high as I could. The end result was … we had *just* enough room for the eight people who were regularly attending. AND BONUS! Because this room was considered an unusable storage room, it wasn't even listed as an available room to be booked in the system! BOOM! We continued on in that room for months, completely left alone. Praise God!

Several months later my team was moved to a different part of the building. My cube was now located in a very high traffic area where folks passed by to get to the restrooms. I decided to use my new prime real estate to let my light shine! I took a couple of the mini posters I had on the inside of my cube and placed them on the outside. My "Before Jesus/After Jesus" poster was getting all kinds of eye hits! Haha! I knew it was a bold move. I also knew that I would go with it until someone said something and then we'd see what happened. Sure enough, about a month later, one of the managers from a different group, who was a believer, came and warned me. She told me that apparently my poster had gotten a few complaints and HR would be advising me to move it from the outside of my cube to the inside.

I had a crossroads moment that day. These grace growers were *really* starting to get under my skin. I couldn't help but think of all the engineers on the same floor that had half naked women all over their cubes in the form of Sport Illustrated calendars. How was my poster "not appropriate" but theirs were? It felt like injustice to me. Later that week my boss personally came over to tell me I had until the end of the week to move it or else there would be repercussions. And, of course, she gave my Bible the death glare on her way out of my cube. That Friday, at the end of the day, I prayed and told the Lord if I get fired over this poster, then I get fired. I walked out of the building fully at peace, prepared to enjoy my weekend.

Monday morning I arrived at work not knowing what to expect. I was stunned as I approached my desk to find my poster was GONE! I was mentally rolling up my sleeve ready to box somebody. When I sat down in my chair and swiveled around, I found the poster up on the inside of my cube and a note from the Christian manager. She expressed that she didn't want me to lose my job over a poster and admitted she moved it for me. I immediately just felt the peace of God. He had used this manager as a covering to protect me. At the end of the day, I was still proud of myself for not budging. My favorite part of this poster story is a few days later Holy Spirit highlighted a spot INSIDE my cube that made the poster more visible than it was when it was on the OUTSIDE! God has the best sense of humor ever!

Side bar: I had several Christian coworkers during this trial who would advise me to "pick my battles" and "just lay low." Here's the thing. The enemy's end game is to wear you out and make you quit! I. AM. NOT. A. QUITTER! So, until the Lord Himself tells me to back off and "pick my battles" and "lay low," you can find me on the frontlines! When you were in school, did you ever witness the kids who gave in to the bully be left alone after that? No! If you're intimidated and back down, the bully is then fully aware he has control over you! I made Jesus Lord of my life and I had no intention of allowing anyone to back me into a corner ever again. Yes, I may get tired. Yes, I may take breaks. But I had resolved years prior that I would *never* quit. Because if you don't quit, you win!

I wish I could say the saga at my workplace ended there, but it didn't. The repositioning of the poster threw my supervisor into even more of a rage against me. One week, out of the blue, she wrote me up and put me on a verbal warning. In my entire career, up until this point, I had never been written up. I was that employee who could always count on a glowing review from my boss when I applied for a new position. My current supervisor cited three things that I failed to do which resulted in customer-impacting errors. I was able to disprove two of the items with emails almost immediately. I had written proof (with date/time stamps) that I had completed both tasks by the deadline. The third item was, in fact, an error on my part, and I took ownership of it. However, that one mistake did not warrant being written up. I knew that and I believe she knew that as well. In our meeting, held to discuss the three items, she completely dismissed my rebuttal on the two items I had disproved and she still asked me to sign the verbal warning. I declined to sign it. Signing that document was an admission that everything in the document was accurate and I was taking full responsibility for it. I was not going to be signing it without revisions being made. Let's just say she leveled up in the rage department when I took my rebuttals above her head.

So, here are at the final two points in this story. Do you need a water break? Bathroom break? More popcorn? I can wait … .

A few weeks after she attempted to write me up, it was time for our annual reviews. I considered myself a good employee. I was honestly bored with the job, and I knew I wasn't perfect. But up until that point in corporate America, I had *never* been written up for anything and I had no intention of allowing this woman to stain my record with nonsense. When it was time for my review, she basically rated me horribly in every area (with no documentation to back up her reasoning). It was strictly an opinion piece. At that point, I'll admit, I started to feel extremely defeated. Picture a fight scene from any of the Rocky movies. I wanted to sit in my corner for a minute and get all the back massages and have water sprayed in my face. I just wanted all my wounds tended to! When was the war with this woman going to end? I was tired of living like this. Every time I'd see her heading my way, I could feel anxiety trying to take over. I sensed the Lord telling me to be at peace, forgive her, and let it go. In this season, I learned so much about loving and praying for my enemies. I did my best to love her and I prayed for her constantly. It was a painful and trying season and there is absolutely no way to gloss over it. I had to fight being overtaken by anger, bitterness, and, honestly, hate.

She ended my annual review by telling me that because of my rating she was not permitted to give me a raise and she actually *smirked* when she said it. It's times like this I've had to remind myself of what Ephesians 6:12 says, "For we do not wrestle against flesh and blood, but against principalities, against powers, against the rulers of the darkness of this age, against spiritual hosts of wickedness in the heavenly places." This woman was being heavily influenced by the enemy and I had to keep reminding myself this was spiritual.

So, I forgave her over and over and eventually I moved on while I continued praying for justice. I even engaged my church family to pray concerning the situation because I was completely over it. Not even a week later, I received a meeting invite from my supervisor. "What now?" was all I could think. Walking into the room, I knew that something was off immediately. She wasn't her typical smug self. She actually looked *very* uncomfortable, which was a new emotion for me to see her wearing. She had a piece of paper turned over in front of her. I just knew something really serious was about to go down. She proceeded to explain to me that our company had hired a third-party consulting/auditing agency to conduct a review of our department and other departments. She explained that they found some major discrepancies among the pay rates and job descriptions. The long and short of it was, this woman who had sabotaged my 3% annual raise was now being forced to give me a 25% raise to bring my pay up to industry standard. You could have pushed me over with a feather!

Guys, God doesn't take it lightly when the enemy (or a person he uses) messes with His kids … He will avenge us. But you know what? We have to keep our Breastplate of Righteousness in place! We have to remain blameless! Sometimes we have to *not* take matters into our own hands. That trial provided many opportunities for me to murmur and complain. And believe me, I had my moments! The urge to vent all over my loved ones was fierce! There were many times when the employees who this supervisor treated like gold would come to me singing her praises. It took everything in me not to correct them and tell them they were deceived about her! I had to learn how to honor her in the midst of the crazy. I touched on praying for her earlier, but it was difficult. However, I obeyed.

One of the last encounters I had with this woman months later was quite bizarre. One morning she snuck up on me. I was on the early shift, so for the first hour or so I was pretty much alone on the floor. She came to my desk and had a seat in the guest chair! Say what now?! That *never* happened. Now mind you, this woman and I never had any chit-chatty types of conversations. It was usually all business.

She sat down and proceeded to tell me how she was having a rough week and an *extremely* rough morning. She explained how she stopped at the gas station that morning on her way in to work and the gas pump she used happened to have a scripture handwritten on it. Apparently the scripture really blessed to her. It was exactly what she needed to hear, given her situation.

Mind you, I feel like I was playing it cool, but for all I know I could have been giving her the crazy side-eye look. I don't know. I knew I should be listening to all the details of this God moment she had just experienced, but I could not get past the "Punk'd" vibes I was getting from this entire exchange. I just knew Ashton Kutcher was going to jump out at any moment! Then she tells me about the "main thing that made the experience extra special." She said it was the handwriting of the verse. This person's handwriting apparently looked like my handwriting and for some reason that was "extra special" to her. I felt like I was in an episode of the Twilight Zone!

I can assure you I was not the one who wrote the scripture she saw on said gas pump. Somehow, for reasons I will NEVER know or understand, the Lord chose to encounter her that way. As I wrote this chapter, the Lord spoke to me Proverbs 16:7, "When people's lives please the LORD, even their enemies are at peace with them."

To this day I wonder why she even hired me. Or maybe she didn't start disliking me until my Bible triggered her. Ultimately the intense spiritual warfare of the entire situation produced the work it was intended to produce in my heart and character (and maybe some others who witnessed it all). It definitely made me grow in the area of righteousness. Apparently, even my "enemy" was impacted for the better.

I'll leave you with this final thought concerning this topic. As you exercise your Breastplate of Righteousness, be encouraged when you encounter the "grace growers." When the enemy fights against us, it's because he sees us as a threat. But as with everything on the Christian journey, anything the enemy means for evil God can and will use it for our good if we allow Him to. My advice is to cling to Genesis 30:33 (NKJV) which tells us, "So my **righteousness** will answer for me in time to come ... ."

Let me pray over you:

> Father, we desire to live righteously because You are righteous. Help us to put our trust in You and have faith in the power of this remarkable armor You have given us. Complete the good work You have begun in us. Let us pursue righteousness all the days of our lives. In Jesus' name!

CHAPTER 8

"Preparation of the Gospel of Peace" Shoes

*N*ow I *know* some of you ladies (and maybe even some of you men) have been waiting to hear about the Gospel Shoes. For no other reason than we're talking about shoes ... just admit it! Did you imagine strappy wedge sandals or leather knee-high boots? Those are my personal faves! But the Shoes of Readiness, the Shoes of the Preparation of the Gospel of Peace, or Gospel Shoes we are unpacking will more than likely not be a pair of strappy wedges, knee high boots, or anything glamorous you may have imagined.

As a matter of fact, the Roman soldier's shoes were often sandals with spikes on them. We're not talking fashion spikes for my punk rock lovers, but spikes on the bottom – like cleats. The purpose of our shoes is to help prepare us to withstand warfare, standing firm (rooted and grounded in our salvation), while also being at complete peace, without fear. These shoes aid us in walking through trials without fear. These shoes help us stand firm in faith! Those spikes have a purpose. These are textured shoes for traction! So we can dig our sandals into whatever terrain we find ourselves in and keep from moving away from God.

So, let's unbox these puppies and walk this out!

I think we can all agree there's a lot to be said about being prepared. The more notice I receive for an event the better, as far as I'm concerned. And God does not want us to be unprepared for any battle we find ourselves in. Like I mentioned in Chapter 1, the second you pledge your life to Christ, you've crossed a very important line of demarcation. You are no longer neutral when it comes to spiritual warfare. You've become an ally of the gospel, which by default makes you an enemy of the devil. His objective is to steal, kill, and destroy anything and everything God loves. Like it or not, there is now a target on your back. But believe it or not, there is no need to fear. Not only are we covered by the blood of Jesus, but God has given us the tools we need to live victoriously. The armor we're studying is just one subset of tools in our armory. We are set up to win! However, the enemy does his best to make you believe otherwise.

Have you ever watched a kid with floaties panic in a pool because they were convinced they were going to drown? Or have you ever witnessed an adult flailing in a pool, convinced they were going to drown, and someone yells to them, "Your feet can touch the bottom!"? Then they straighten up and, albeit embarrassed, they "save" themselves? I've seen both in action. And I may or may not have been the adult once, so there's that. These are great illustrations of what the enemy does to us. He tries to convince us the world is ending and we're all going die.

I remember early in my Christian walk hearing a pastor explain fear as an acronym:

<u>F</u>alse
<u>E</u>vidence
<u>A</u>ppearing
<u>R</u>eal

That sermon would be one I'd refer to many, many times over the next several years of my life. The devil is a liar. We've got to get hip to the game and stop his lies dead in their tracks. Next step? Rise above and see past the smoke and mirrors. These Gospel Shoes of Peace are going to help us do just that.

In high school I was what teachers referred to as both right-brained and left-brained. While I adored the arts, music, band, and literature (right brain), I also *loved* math and science (left brain). Physics may have been my favorite science of them all – possibly because it combined both math and science. My favorite physics principle was: For every action there is an equal and opposite reaction. This is Newton's third law of Physics.

In studying the Gospel Shoes, I felt like there was a duality to the shoes. I mean we're talking about preparation of the gospel, but then again, we're also talking about peace. I had to keep mulling it over to see how the two really came together. As believers, there is no question that we're supposed to be sharing the gospel. We always need to be prepared to share the gospel. However, at the same time, sharing the gospel is an offensive strike where the kingdom of darkness is concerned and, therefore, there's likely going to be some pushback – spiritual warfare if you will.

An equal and opposite reaction? Well, no, not in this case. Because we all know the enemy is no match for God. It may not be equal, but there *will* be an opposite reaction. When the warfare comes, what do we need most? Depending on the circumstances, that answer may vary. However, *peace* can't hurt! We need to stand firm and hold our ground with a mindset of peace. Remember the spikes on the bottom of the sandals? They help us to stay grounded and brace ourselves against any onslaught that comes our way. We take ground, the enemy tries to push back, we stand our ground … rinse … repeat! BOOM!

Several months back, I had the opportunity to talk to a new believer. Since he was just about as loquacious as I was, we wound up talking for hours concerning his new Christian walk. At one point in the conversation, he began to express his deep desire to help people. But his passion gave way to frustration when he admitted he didn't even know how to share the gospel. An idea began to hatch in my mind. I gave him a few pointers on evangelizing, however, I was working on a surprise for the next time we ran into each other.

In my lifetime, I've only been on about six international mission trips. I hope to do many more in the future. I've had the opportunity to go to Guatemala twice, Peru, Venezuela, Israel, and during the 2004 Olympics I joined a team doing street and sports evangelism in Greece. Many times as we broke out into groups, we didn't have a translator. We knew we would have to rely heavily on Holy Spirit to even get a conversation going due to the language barrier. We needed to get creative. In preparing for one of these trips, I was introduced to the Evangecube. It's a tool about the size of a Rubix cube that serves as a visual presentation of the gospel. There are no words on the cube so the message transcends any language. Google it. It's pretty amazing.

The next time I met with this new Christian, I presented the Evangecube to him. I demonstrated how to use it. I presented the gospel to him twice and then handed it over to him and said, "Now it's your turn." He definitely was not expecting that. So once his wide eyes went back to their normal size, he accepted the challenge and presented the gospel to me. I cannot even begin to explain the feeling of pride I had, but what moved me the most was how the experience impacted him. This not so quiet guy was *shook*. In a matter of five minutes, we were able to completely eliminate one of his greatest frustrations.

I encouraged him by telling him that once he had shared the gospel a few times, he wouldn't really need the cube, not in the US anyway. Haha! I'm a visual learner, so the pictures are seared into my mind's eye. It happens the same way for many others as well.

Be prepared. Be prepared with the preparation of the gospel of peace. People need to hear this gospel and meet the person behind it. Jesus is life changing. Shoot, He is the way, the truth, and the life! Jesus saves, transforms, resets, redeems, and upgrades so many lives. We can't keep Him a secret!

First Peter 3:15b says, "And if someone asks about your hope as a believer, always be ready to explain it."

Continuing on with the story, the best surprise came about three days later. After sharing the cube with this new believer, I received one of the best voicemail messages ever! He explained how the next day he went to pick up his five-year-old son for the weekend. He was so excited he shared the Evangecube with his son and taught him how to share the gospel himself. I listened to the rest of the voicemail with my jaw practically on the floor and tears welled up in my eyes. He reported that when he dropped off his son back at his mother's Sunday afternoon, the first thing his son wanted to do was share the gospel with his grandpa, his grandma, and his mother. His son literally went to each one of them, one by one, and shared the gospel with them using the Evangecube! Say whaaaaaaaat!?

In a matter of three days, a man feeling defeated about not being able to share his faith learned how, taught his son, and his son turned right around and evangelized the rest of his family! I lost count of how many times I replayed that voice message.

But in his usual fashion, later that *same day,* the enemy came after this new believer hard and he started to be derailed from what God was calling him to. You see, this new believer had shared with me how God had been revealing to him the direction his life should be going in. He'd been faithful to take the appropriate steps to pursue God and begin to sever ties from his old lifestyle. The same night that he'd shared the testimony concerning this son he had asked for prayer to sever one final old relationship. His plan was to meet up with this person and explain he was moving in a new direction. However, the end result was that this person was able to convince this new believer to stay in the relationship. Him staying eventually led to him completely backsliding in his walk and becoming estranged from the Lord. He became a prodigal. I pray every day that the blood of Jesus would reconcile this man back to his original design, purpose, function, and destiny. We *must* be prepared for warfare. We don't have to be afraid of it, but we have to be alert!

First Peter 5:8 reminds us, "Stay alert! Watch out for your great enemy, the devil. He prowls around like a roaring lion, looking for someone to devour." We have got to learn how to stand our ground. My prayer for you is Ephesians 3:17b, that "your roots will grow down into God's love and keep you strong."

The bottom line is we're in a war, a spiritual war of epic proportions. As counterintuitive as it seems, we can still be victorious and maintain our peace. I love the way Joyce Meyer says it in her YouTube video titled "Walking in the Shoes of Peace:"

> You can't just sit around praying for peace. I pray that you realize that God's already given you peace and that you do

what you need to do to walk in it. A lot of times we keep asking God to give us something we've already got! What we need to do is use what Jesus has already given us. He said peace I give you! Now you stop letting yourself getting all disturbed and upset.

So how do we keep our peace? I'm so glad you asked! You keep your peace by remaining in Him and exercising your God-given authority. So, what does remaining in Him look like? One of my favorite passages in the Bible is John 15:4-8, which is about abiding and remaining in God:

> Remain in me, and I will remain in you. For a branch cannot produce fruit if it is severed from the vine, and you cannot be fruitful unless you remain in me. "Yes, I am the vine; you are the branches. Those who remain in me, and I in them, will produce much fruit. For apart from me you can do nothing. Anyone who does not remain in me is thrown away like a useless branch and withers. Such branches are gathered into a pile to be burned. But if you remain in me and my words remain in you, you may ask for anything you want, and it will be granted! When you produce much fruit, you are my true disciples. This brings great glory to my Father.

Remaining in Him looks like spending time with Him. Spending time can look like reading the Word, praying for others, worshipping, sitting and listening and recording what He speaks to you. You may think, "Recording what He speaks? Sounds a bit extreme." Remember the enemy comes to steal. I can't tell you how many times God speaks revelation to my friends and I have to remind them of what He told them. It happens the other way around, too. Several times I'd be asking the same question of God and a friend would come in and say, "Didn't you say He told you *xyz* about that?" Record it. Journal it. Write it down so you can go back and review what He said.

You guys, full transparency here. No joke! There are days I have very early quiet times with the Lord and I write down what He says. Later that evening I go back and reread it and it's like I'm reading someone else's notes! The hustle and bustle of one day is enough to make you forget what He spoke earlier in the day. Do not rely on your memory! I also love when I look back on the things I recorded years ago and the same message is speaking to my current situation. He's amazing that way!

Abiding can also be singing scripture, praying in the spirit, repenting for sin … the list goes on and on. Be led by the Spirit. Do what you feel led to do, but CONNECT, ABIDE, and REMAIN! Have a relationship. He wants to be Your Father, not a checklist. The bottom line is stay connected. Stay connected to Him. He's the source of everything good. About ten years ago He called me to take a vacation with Him. I literally drove six hours to the beach by myself for a week. It was a little awkward at first – not even gonna lie. But a couple of days in, this busy extrovert was able to chill and sit with her Father. The Martha in me gave way to Mary (Luke 10:38-42), and it is one of my favorite and most peaceful memories to date!

Earlier I spoke about using your authority. What does this look like?

Proverbs 18:21 puts it this way: "The tongue has the power of life and death." I personally like to identify what the enemy is attacking with and find scripture that declares the opposite … the TRUTH!

So, let's say the enemy is trying to convince you that the infirmity or sickness you have is just your lot in life, and you're never going to get healed. What's your next move? I hope it isn't to wallow in self-pity and agree with him! Remember, he's a liar! I am baffled by how many people do the enemy's work for him by speaking all kinds of nonsense over themselves. A great next step would be to find a ton of scripture about healing which is your right, portion, and inheritance as a child of God! Speak those scriptures over yourself daily! Take your authority. There is POWER in your tongue. Use it.

Scripture: Isaiah 53:5 (NRSV)
"But he was wounded for our transgressions, crushed for our iniquities; upon him was the punishment that made us whole, and by his bruises we are healed."

Declaration: Thank You Jesus that by Your bruises I am healed. I appropriate Your sacrifice to my physical body and receive my healing in Jesus' Name!

Scripture/Declaration: Jeremiah 17:14 (ESV)
"Heal me, O Lord, and I shall be healed; save me, and I shall be saved; for you are my praise."

Put on your shoes my friends! Be prepared to share the gospel and exercise your authority to stay in a place of peace.

Father, I thank You that Peace is our portion as we take on sharing the gospel of Jesus. We will not be deterred! We will stand our ground. As we remain in You, You will prepare us for every obstacle on our path. We will not turn our backs on the gospel. Strengthen us to do the work You've called us to do. In Jesus' Name I pray. Amen!

CHAPTER 9

Putting on the Shoes of the Preparation of the Gospel of Peace

For shoes, put on the peace that comes from
the Good News so that you will be fully prepared.
Ephesians 6:15

Many years ago, I had the opportunity to join a team of people heading to Guatemala for a mission trip that I mentioned in the last chapter. This was my first mission trip ever and I was beyond stoked! We spent months discussing logistics: dates, lodging, strategy, and itinerary. We even took classes on how to be culturally sensitive. We made sure to discuss the things that were considered offensive to the people we would be ministering to, like pointing, showing the bottom of our shoes, and being too loud.

Most of the team was a little nervous as it was the first mission trip we would be going on. For months leading up to the trip, we tried to learn some native K'ekchi' which was a Mayan language spoken by the people group we would be ministering to. We all had raised funds for our trip via support letters and shopped for appropriate clothing in preparation. All in all, we were buzzing with excitement. This was an act of obedience for just about all of us. During some of our team meetings, we had the privilege of sharing with one another why we felt called to this trip. It was a wonderful time of preparation and bonding.

At the time of the trip, I was part of a church which hosted multiple international mission trips every year. As a matter of fact, we hosted a Mission Conference every year, with a table set up for every country that had a scheduled mission trip. We had the opportunity to move around the room and pray, asking God if we were to participate in any of the trips, and asking Him specifically where He wanted us to go. The "Here am I! Send me!" force was very strong at this church!

There was a very strong sense of calling among the team members. Unfortunately, as with any international mission trip, the "doom and gloom prophets" also come along who want to explain to us all the reasons we shouldn't go. 'Cause you know, apparently they're the only ones with access to the *spirit of the evening news*. At the end of the day, everyone is not going to be onboard with what has God called you to do, and that's their problem, not yours. You just continue to walk in obedience and press forward.

Side Bar. Are you familiar with the story of Nehemiah? Well, it can be found in the Book of … Nehemiah. You're welcome. I'm here to help.

I'm going give you the Cassandra cliff notes version also known as the NCV (New Cassandra Version). I know, I know. I've been verbally sharing it for years now. It's probably high time for it to hit print! Anywho … Nehemiah. He was a servant of King Artaxerxes back during one of the many times the Israelites went into captivity. One day he heard news that the Jews were returning from captivity. However, they were not doing well and their walls were in ruins. Nehemiah prayed, wept, fasted, and mourned before God. Eventually, with the King's permission, he takes a leave of absence and sets out on a mission to rebuild the walls of Jerusalem.

Some of the King's officials were not happy with this idea. One of the main officials, Sandballot, openly opposed Nehemiah and his efforts. He started off by mocking the Jews for rebuilding, attempting to make them feel like their efforts were useless. When that didn't work, Nehemiah 4:8

says, "They all made plans to come and fight against Jerusalem and throw [them] into confusion."

With every step of opposition, Nehemiah and his crew prayed to God for protection. Sandballot and his crew continued to scheme and even tried to set up Nehemiah in an ambush masked as a meeting. Nehemiah, hip to the game, declines four times! At one point, Sandballot hired hecklers. You guys! He hired hecklers to literally ridicule the workers, day and night, as they were building, to discourage them and make them quit! The enemy is persistent. What are you going to do about it?

You can be certain that whatever God calls you to is going to come with some kind of opposition. That statement shouldn't make you feel discouraged; it should make you feel like it's time for preparation. There's a difference. It's nice that we have weather forecasts that can give us the opportunity to prepare for rain. It's so convenient that we can launch a GPS app to get a heads-up about traffic or accidents that could affect our ETA. It's always better to be prepared than to be caught unawares.

Now back to the Guatemala mission team. Many of us had a strong sense of calling and no hecklers were about to derail us. I remember feeling such a sense of camaraderie and purpose with these guys. We all knew there was risk and danger involved, but the sense of calling far surpassed any of that. At the same time, many of us were experiencing spiritual warfare in our personal lives leading up to the trip. Every single time someone shared the latest obstacle that had erupted in their lives, we'd gather around them and pray. We knew what this was and we weren't backing down. So the enemy stepped up his game, just like he had Sandballot do in Nehemiah's life.

It was about a week before we were scheduled to leave for our trip when *major* civil unrest broke out in Guatemala. I can't remember another time when I saw Guatemala in the evening news so much. Every news station was showing footage of pickup trucks filled with men armed with machine guns. These were civilians, not the military! The streets were full of these trucks. Cars were on fire. Alarms were going off! People were rioting! The enemy had launched a level 1000 fear bomb attack. Well played, devil, well played.

The fear and anxiety level had reached such a peak that the leaders of the mission trip, both domestically and internationally, called everyone into an emergency meeting. For about 20 minutes we were briefed on the civil unrest and how it would affect our trip if we still wanted to go. Once the debriefing was over, there seemed to be what felt like 20 minutes of silence. The air was steeped in anxiety and uncertainty – probably the same spirit of unrest that had been launched upon the nation of Guatemala.

I remember sitting in that room, in the silence, with a million thoughts running through my head. Am I called to be a martyr? Are they going to cancel the trip if too many people back out? Are these machine gun-armed civilians hostile towards foreigners? Does this mean I won't get to try those delicious Guatemalan meals they've been showing us pictures of for months?!? Okay, focus Cassandra. Man, how much God must love the K'ekchi' Indian people! And consequently, how fearful the enemy must be of these K'ekchi' Indian people and the work we were planning to accomplish with them. What are the odds that all this unrest erupts *a week* before we're supposed to leave?! What in the world did you sign me up for, Papa?!

See, I was on to the enemy and his schemes. I already knew this was some high-level warfare. I knew in my heart I was called to this, and I felt that supernatural peace that surpasses all understanding the Bible speaks of. In my mind, I dug my heels deeper into the ground. I wasn't backing out! But the question was, who else on my team was still going to go in light of all this?

This was the moment of truth! We can say, "Here am I! Send me!" 'til the cows come home, but this is where the rubber meets the road. Talk is cheap! Everyone's full of faith until they're faced with a truck full of civilians with machine guns! I was very curious to see what became of the "God called me to this" confessions of my teammates. After the longest pause *ever*, one of our leaders stood up and shared his heart from a personal perspective. He shared that he knew this was a hard decision. Some of the people in the room had kids. Some people were the sole breadwinner in their family. There was no guarantee of safety and he wanted everyone to know there was no condemnation if anyone decided to back out. Then he asked for a show of hands of all the people who were still willing to go. Cue the dramatic superhero music!

My heart was pounding! I knew my answer, and it was solid. But the moment just carried so much intensity. I watched with tears in my eyes as every single person in that room raised they hands in unison. No stragglers. No undecideds. Every single person raised their hands at the same time, agreeing to move forward! And guess what? A week later we all boarded the plane, shared the gospel more times than I could count, got invited into so many indigenous huts, and were offered so many questionable homemade drinks which I pretended to sip on. Big shout out to a teammate who drank most of mine for me. We were trained that we shouldn't refuse anything we were offered to eat or drink, as it was considered an insult. His bravery came at a cost though ... in the form of Motezuma's Revenge. Obedience comes with a cost! Bwahahahahahahah!

In all seriousness, my friends, these shoes shod in the preparation of the Gospel of Peace are powerful! They will accomplish the purpose they were intended to. God wouldn't give us junk armor and send us into war. I can't think of one time when fear hit me on the trip. He gave me His peace and I believe he did the same thing for every person on the team as well. Trust His mission! Trust His equipping! Put on your shoes and trust that the victory is yours!

CHAPTER 10

Shield of Faith

What a fun unboxing! Belts, breastplates, shoes ... what's next!? Yeah, well the title of the chapter already gave it away, so whatever! Let's get to it.

Wow, this shield is ginormous. I'm kind of getting that Mary Poppin's vibe when she starts pulling all of that craziness out of her purse. Do you remember when she pulled a coat rack out of her purse, which was sitting on the table? One of my favorite parts of that movie was when the kid looked under the table like, "what kind of magic is that!?"

Okay, let's head back over to our Roman soldier. In this day and age of superhero movies, we don't really need to go into great depth explaining the purpose of a shield. However, I'm going to touch on it briefly anyway. The shield was obviously used for the protection of the soldier – to block and protect him from any form of attack. Spiritually, Paul tells us the purpose of our shield is to "stop the fiery arrows of the devil."

Ephesian 6:16 in its entirety says, "In addition to all of these, <u>hold up the shield of faith</u> to stop the fiery arrows of the devil." (Underlining is mine.) Interesting, isn't it? Did you catch the subtlety there? *Faith* will stop the fiery darts of the enemy *if* we hold the shield up. You see, faith is not this passive Girl Scout patch you just iron onto your shirt, like flare, and expect it to magically do something for you. No shade, Scouts. Love the cookies, by the way.

So, what is faith? According to Webster's dictionary, "Faith is complete trust or confidence in someone or something." According to Hebrews 11:1 (NKJV), "Faith is the substance of things hoped for, the evidence of things not seen."

Think of faith as a verb. Faith is action! Faith has no middle ground. Faith isn't wishy washy. Faith is not complacent. Is your shield up or down? You're either activating it or you're not, right? Based on Ephesians 6:16, the fiery darts are coming either way, so we need to assess how we are activating our faith in this battle.

I personally find that my faith is most tested in the seasons when God is calling me to *wait* on His timing. Especially when it comes to waiting on God's promises. A ton of things can happen in the waiting period:

- The fiery darts of *doubt* come at you whispering, "Did you really hear Him correctly?"
- The fiery darts of *lies* come, "It's never going to happen."
- The fiery darts of *despair*, "Nothing is ever going to change!"
- The fiery darts of *shame*, "You can't step into your calling after everything you've done."
- The fiery darts of *comparison*, "Wow. Look how much more accomplished and successful they are than you are!"

And even more *lies*, "God has completely forgotten about you. Are you still holding out on that pipe dream?"

The devil doesn't have any new tricks. He's not the Creator. So he recycles the same stuff until he finds something you'll fall for. The lies and the "did God really say ... " ridicule are the same tricks he pulled on Eve in the Garden of Eden, remember?

I have a personal story that will help illustrate. I have a friend who tells me that she can listen to my God stories all day long because they are so crazy. I'm that girl who tells my God stories and the usual response is "WOW! You really can't make this stuff up."

I'll be the first to tell you, waiting on the Lord is hard. It's one of the hardest things He asks me to do. I'm a Type A personality. I'm a mover and a shaker. I'm an Enneagram 7. Right!? However, I also don't know when my faith muscles get a better workout than in those seasons of waiting. It pains me to admit that, but it's the undeniable truth. Then when the appointed time arrives and God is ready to put His plans into full swing, it's stunning and leaves me speechless every single time. No one writes a story like my God.

I was reflecting the other day about all the jobs I've had since college. Every single job was acquired by some kind of supernatural means, a divine connection initiated by God or a "random" reconnecting with a friend or acquaintance. He has been faithful to make a way my entire career.

In one particular season, I had been praying for a new job. Specifically, I was praying for a work-from-home job and a certain salary. I started hearing some very encouraging testimonies of people with similar backgrounds who were at similar stations in life securing jobs paying far more than I had the faith to pray for. With those testimonies, scales fell off of my eyes. I realized my shield was not up all the way! Fiery darts of lies were hitting me repeatedly:

- "You'll never land a job like that."
- "You won't even get an interview."
- "People like you never make it that far up the food chain."
- "Your resume isn't strong enough."
- "You can only land a job like that through nepotism. You're just not that well connected."

I decided something needed to change. The very end of James 4:2 (NASB) says, "You do not have because you do not ask." I was convicted and came to the conclusion I needed to activate my faith!

I was bored with the job I currently had. To make matters worse, there was no room for job growth or career-pathing in this small company I was with. I teamed up with a prayer warrior friend and we started warring in prayer for a job breakthrough in both of our lives. We faithfully prayed every weekday during our lunch breaks. We were unrelenting and I was full of faith that I would land the job I was asking for. Shields up!

I want to point out that fiery darts can also come from people in your circle, too. The enemy will use anything and anyone to get to you. I distinctly remember heading downtown to see a show with someone in my circle. We hadn't seen each other in a while, so we were playing a mean game of catch-up on the ride over. She asked me how things were going at work. I explained to her that I felt like my season on my current job was coming to an end. I started sharing with her the type of job I had set my sights on. I was probably high on hope, talking a mile a minute, and extremely enthusiastic about my new goal.

When I was done, she looks over at me and says, "That's going to be hard to accomplish without XYZ in your background and on your resume." And I came crashing down.

Lesson #1. In this battle, we've got to learn who the *safe* people are we can share our hopes and dreams with. Not everyone has faith for what you have faith for. Not everyone trusts God the way you do. And let's face it, not everyone is for you. It's a hard truth but not everyone is excited for you when you succeed.

Lesson #2. People are in different places in their own walks with the Lord. Some are not really walking with Him at all. Sometimes people project their own fears and failures on you because they haven't dealt with their own junk. It's funny to me, that out of the million things I shared with this person, she honed in on the one qualification I was missing, which incidentally was the same one she was missing.

She was projecting. The Lord had to point out to me that she had allowed herself to be hindered and held back in her own career because she believed the lie. She had literally just revealed to me the exact fiery dart that had kept her stuck for years (whether she realized it or not). I really felt like the Lord was speaking to me, "… and I have opened a door for you that no one can close" (Revelation 3:8). That was all I needed to hear! Once I fully processed all that, I was able to wipe her words right out of my mind like a windshield wiper and move on with my life. What's for me, is for me! Onward and upward!

So back to the job search! One day I had a recruiter reach out to me presenting a job opportunity that was seemingly perfect! I jumped through all the hoops and went through all the interviews. Both the hiring manager and the recruiter felt I was a shoo-in for the position. However, days went by after the final interview. Days turned into weeks. I tried emailing and calling this recruiter and never heard back. Eventually, I took it upon myself to reach out to the hiring manager to find out what was going on. When we connected, he was shocked to hear I hadn't received an update. He quickly explained to me that due to some company politics he was forced to promote someone from within instead of hiring someone from the outside.

I was completely devastated! I felt like God had promised me a work-from-home job at the salary this company was willing to offer me. Lots of tears of frustration were shed. Not many things are worse than being on the cusp of a breakthrough and having it ripped out from underneath you. Between my disappointment and the taunting of the enemy, I had to work extra hard to not get into a place of bitterness. I had to work even harder to continue to have faith that I would receive what I was praying for and what God promised me.

Practical application: That looks like praying while reminding God what He promised you. That looks like declaring scriptures like: The Lord will make me the head and not the tail, and I will always be on top and never at the bottom. (Deuteronomy 28:13)

I clung to one of my favorite prayer books in this season. It's called *Prayer Rain* and it's by Dr. Olukoya, a minister in Nigeria. You can easily find it on Amazon. Listen, I have the hard cover version at home and the leather bound (thinner copy) for my purse! Yes, I would go everywhere with that thing! When I had any spare time, I would bust out one of his prayers (which are mostly scriptures) and I would declare and decree till I could decree no more!

In the waiting, there were many times I felt like I was losing my hope. You could say that my shield of faith was starting to droop. Almost a year went by and I was still wounded by the entire experience. But throughout the whole year, following that debacle, I felt like the Lord kept reminding me to trust Him. He was reminding me that His promises are yes and amen.

He was promising that anything that had been stolen from me would be returned to me, as an upgrade, too. Sign me up!

Seemingly, out of the blue, another recruiter contacted me almost a year later. However, due to my simply being over the last experience, I ignored him for about a week until finally the Lord convicted my heart. He told me that instead of ignoring the recruiter I should at the very least reach out to him and let him know I was not interested in the position. Fair enough. I decided to give him a call. I mean, what could it hurt? While speaking with the recruiter, I made it clear that I would not be leaving my current job unless a phenomenal opportunity came my way and made it worth my while. I wasn't playing it shy this time around. I made it clear I wasn't interested in a lateral move either. I also was not interested in a nominal raise. I seriously wonder sometimes why that guy even continued talking to me. Haha! I was playing total hardball with him, hoping he would give up, honestly.

Then came the moment of truth when he asked me this very pivotal question, "What would it take for you to consider taking on the job with this company?" I got a little sassy with it. I gave him a crazy salary that was $10K above the salary the last company was offering me. I told him I wanted to work from home at least three days a week. I also told him securing a job with a company that paid out bonuses was a top priority for me. What did I have to lose, right? I wasn't really interested at that point and, in retrospect, it was probably me trying to protect myself from what happened before. So imagine my surprise when the recruiter responded with, "I think we can make all of that happen!" Not even going to lie, it took me a minute to recover! Even better, he said I could work from home four days a week. What the whaaaaaaat!?

So I went through all the interviews. Every single one felt like I was having a casual chat with some new friends. The ease, grace, and favor of the Lord was off the charts. The Lord completely smoothed a path for me to waltz right in and somehow blinded them to the fact that, on paper, I was technically under qualified. Haha! A few days after my final interview, I was offered the job officially. Within two weeks I had worked my resignation notice and was on my way out of state for training!

In a year, I had secured a better job, with better pay and better benefits than the original job I was being offered. And you want to hear something even crazier? The main distributor for the original company filed for bankruptcy a year after I started at my new job. The Lord works in mysterious ways. We just have to commit to keeping our faith high, no matter the circumstances. Keeping our faith high means we stop coming into agreement with what the negative voices around us are speaking, too.

Speaking of voices, when we find ourselves in difficult seasons, we have to surround ourselves with things that bring life! Things that will cause our faith to rise! Release worship into your home. When things get crazy, I have Pandora playing worship music 24/7 around here. Instead binging on news, I binge on what the prophetic voices are saying. I subscribe to the The Elijah List, a site whose purpose it is to give trustworthy, daily prophetic worship and intercessory "content" to as many believers (and even unbelievers) as possible. I sign up for daily encouragement to hit my email box.

Take inventory of your life. What are the things that cause faith to rise in you? Is it sermons from your favorite preachers? Hanging with friends who speak life over you? I challenge you right now to make a list. What are the five things that cause faith to rise in your life? My five things are (in no particular order):

1. Worship music.
2. Praying prayers out of *Prayer Rain.*
3. Fellowshipping with fiery friends who speak life and always have a testimony on their lips.
4. Listening to encouraging sermons/preaching.
   a. When Kim Clement was alive I faithfully tuned in to all of his services and they changed me.
   b. These days I try to tune into everything happening at Glory of Zion, Chuck Pierce's ministry in Texas.
   c. On Instagram, I love catching the Steven Furtick posts.
5. Reading my prophetic words over and over!

Solidify your strategy now, because the middle of the battle is not the best time to figure out what you should be doing. Can God give us strategy in the midst? Absolutely! But be as prepared as you can be. My friends, let faith arise!

CHAPTER 11

Putting on the Shield of Faith

*In addition to all of these, hold up the shield of
faith to stop the fiery arrows of the devil.*
Ephesians 6:16

*G*rowing up I always had a flair for the dramatic. (I see all you people in my personal circle nodding. LOL!) I love movies! I love to sing! I love musicals! I love to dance! I was even on a drill team. Pom pom puffs on my white Keds and all. Yep, I was too cool for school. In junior high (that's middle school for my southern friends) and high school, I was in just about every single musical. I was in the marching band all throughout high school. And although I played the flute in the orchestra band, I was part of the color guard in the marching band. I even served as color guard co-captain my senior year in high school. Performing arts is a life-long passion of mine. I was created for it.

After high school, I had a talent agent for a short stint. I did some extra work in a bunch of random commercials and low budget movies here in the Atlanta area. That was all long before Atlanta became the second Hollywood. After so many extra stints, I got a little discouraged. I felt like I was doing what I was supposed to be doing, however I wasn't seeing a tremendous amount of fruit from it.

One weekend in 1999, my talent agency announced that the International Model & Talent Association was coming to Atlanta on a nationwide search for fresh talent. Winners would be sent to Los Angeles for a national competition and that alone could provide some very promising leads. While my director couldn't have been more excited for me to audition, I was on the fence. Although I was passionate about the entertainment industry, I knew that Hollywood wasn't for the faint of heart. I was experiencing a lot of doubt about whether I should press forward or hang my hat altogether. I didn't look like a Barbie doll. I didn't have any connections. The amount of money in my bank account wasn't even enough to get a kid excited about a shopping spree at Dollar Tree. I basically didn't have much going for me except my passion. However, I knew if God wanted this for me, then He would show me and make a way.

With all this competition business, I decided to lay out a fleece. What's a fleece you say? Great question, class! Gideon and his fleece is one of my favorite Bible stories. I know … I have a lot of favorites. It is what it is. So let me preface this story. Once again the NCV (New Cassandra Version) is coming atcha!

The Angel of the Lord pretty much rolls up on Gideon, who's minding his own business handling his 9-5, threshing wheat. The Angel of the Lord calls Gideon to lead an army of men into battle to rescue Israel outta some nonsense. Gideon is like, "Say whaaaaaaat, Sir!? Me? Naw!" Angel of the Lord is like, "I got you!" Gideon's probably giving Him the side eye (there's no biblical evidence of that, but, you know). The Angel of the Lord continues gassing up Gideon. Finally, the Angel of the Lord is like, "Bruh! I'm going to be RIGHT. THERE. WITH. YOU! You're gonna win!" Gideon's like, "Prove it, my man!" (Even though He really wasn't a man … but you're tracking with me, right?)

Okay. So Gideon prepares an offering and brings it back to the Angel of the Lord. The Angel of the Lord tells him to put all the items on the rock so he can prove all that He'd said and promised. Angel of the Lord is not playing games, so He whips out an epic miracle, the kind pyromaniacs' dreams are made of, and burns it all up with the tip of His staff. I wouldn't be surprised if He then gave Gideon an "Are we settled here, my dude?" look. However, the Bible doesn't give us any camera close-up shots on this scene, so we'll never really know for sure. Gideon decides to believe the Angel of the Lord, finally, and sets out on his mission. Now let's fast forward to the fleece.

The battle is full on and now Gideon's enemies are forming alliances left and right. Gideon is starting to question the entire mission once again. I'll let the NLT version of the Bible take it from here. Judges 6:36-40:

> Then Gideon said to God, "If you are truly going to use me to rescue Israel as you promised, prove it to me in this way. I will put a wool fleece on the threshing floor tonight. If the fleece is wet with dew in the morning but the ground is dry, then I will know that you are going to help me rescue Israel as you promised." And that is just what happened. When Gideon got up early the next morning, he squeezed the fleece and wrung out a whole bowlful of water.

> Then Gideon said to God, "Please don't be angry with me, but let me make one more request. Let me use the fleece for one more test. This time let the fleece remain dry while the ground around it is wet with dew." So that night God did as Gideon asked. The fleece was dry in the morning, but the ground was covered with dew.

That is bad to the bone! I don't care what anybody says! I could totally relate to Gideon. God was calling him to do something that was daunting and literally impossible in his own strength! He had nothing to hang on to other than his faith in who God was and what God was speaking to him. I ended up doing something very similar. I had a conversation with God and sensed very strongly that I was supposed to attend the competition. I was afraid it would somehow be a waste of time and resources, but I went anyway out of obedience.

Upon arriving, I listened while the head judge explained the rules of the competition. There were basically going to be multiple rounds of the competition, just like an American Idol type of show. They would continue to narrow down the contestants until they had a certain number in each category. The competition was broken up into age categories, and then further into categories like modeling, acting, singing, and dancing. The head judge explained that we'd each have an opportunity to audition. He advised, after we auditioned, we'd just have to wait to see if we got a callback. He started to walk away when he suddenly turned on his heels and came back to center stage. He says something to the effect of, "Oh, I forgot to mention! In the off chance that your audition is so astounding that you get a raving review from each judge, you will receive a WHITE CARD. Receiving a white card means you get to bypass the rest of the audition process and, in essence, receive an instant ticket to the LA competition." You could hear the collection of gasps and whispers in the room, which was immediately squashed by him saying, "But that rarely ever happens." And off he went to his seat.

And there it was! My fleece! My sign! Right then and there I started a conversation with God. I said, "Papa! I know this is my passion but I don't even want to do it anymore if You're not going to go before me. The odds are too heavily stacked against me. As painful as it is to say, I'm willing to lay all of this down today. If You're saying that the entertainment industry is a calling that You've placed on my life, then I want that white card TUH-DAY. I don't want to come back for more auditions. Make it plain, make it clear." Yup! I got real bold with it. I went for broke.

My turn to audition came and I had prepared a comedic monologue. I gave that monologue my all! Then I stood there and stared at the three judges and they stared at me. I felt like I was going to throw up. The first judge speak ups and says something like, "That was pretty remarkable!" I almost passed out! But I couldn't get ahead of myself. I reminded the Lord, "I want that white card if You're *really* calling me to the entertainment industry!" I stood there for what felt like three years. It was like everything was happening in slow motion. I seriously don't even remember what the second guy said, but I remember he had a big smile on his face while he nodded. I interpreted it as, "Impressive." Then the final head judge says very matter of factly, "Well, look at that! The first white card of the day! See you in LA!" When I screamed, he cracked a smile and I was out the door!

Say whaaaaaaaaaaaaaat!?? It's been 20 years since that all happened, so I honestly cannot even remember if I ugly cried, blacked out, or what. There was something much bigger happening than winning a ticket to LA for the national competition! God just answered my FLEECE! Just call me Gideona! LOL. I went to that competition in LA and guess what? I won first place in the national sitcom competition for my age group. God wasn't playing around. He was making it abundantly clear that I'd heard Him correctly the first time and that the plan had not changed.

You may ask … so what have you done in the entertainment industry since 2000? NOTHING! Haha! Well, to be honest, I had a few more gigs as an extra, but nothing worth going into great detail about. Except the one time, while walking through a Blockbuster Video store, I saw that my picture ended up on the back cover of the VHS for a locally-made movie I had a supporting role in forever ago! I purposely share this story because it's a testimony that is *still* in the making! I have been holding up my Shield of Faith in this area since January of 2000! It's been over 20 years! Have I lost faith? Nope! Do I think it's too late? Nope! Have the fiery darts of the enemy come at me constantly trying to convince me to give up on that dream? Fo sho!

Now I will say this, my dream may not be fulfilled the way I envisioned it way back in 2000. He never told me *where* I would wind up in the entertainment industry, He just told me I would. Back then, I envisioned national commercials, sitcom roles, and maybe some movie roles. These days I dream about voiceover work, writing songs for musical artists, writing for TV shows, and maybe even possibly hosting a TV show … who knows!? However, when the time comes, I'll be ready. I haven't wavered once and I don't intend to start now.

I don't want to minimize the Shield of Faith to just believing for a dream to be fulfilled. That can be part of it, but it's so much more than that! This Faith Shield we're rocking represents everything we believe about God, who He says He is, and what He's said He will do! And if He said it, He will do it! When the enemy shoots those fiery darts of lies and intimidation at you, *lift up your shield.*

Sometimes, I imagine that on the inside of the Shield of Faith are the words God spoke to/over us. Those promises He made through His words in the Bible and other prophetic words given through the saints. I imagine sometimes that it's a list of all the things we're hoping for, those things we have yet to see but have complete confidence will manifest. Read your own list of things hoped for, and then read it again while you're holding your shield up.

Open up your mouth and make declarations! What has He promised us? What has He promised you?

God, we thank You that Your promises are "Yes and amen!" Second Corinthians 1:20 (NIV) says, "For no matter how many promises God has made, they are '**Yes**' in Christ. And so through him the '**Amen**' is spoken by us to the glory of God."

If that didn't make you want to shout, then … SHOUT NOW ANYWAY! Let every fiery dart be extinguished as we stand in Faith! Shields up! Mouths open, reminding Him of His promises and sealing them with an AMEN!

We will not be shaken! We will not be crushed by fiery darts! Father, make us faithful sons and daughters because You are a Faithful Father!

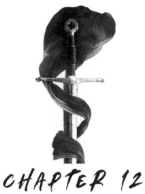

CHAPTER 12

Helmet of Salvation

We are back to our unboxing! I must say I'm thoroughly enjoying this and I hope that you are, too. Sometimes when we're faced with daunting tasks it helps to break things into segments. That's what we've been doing here. Tackling each piece of armor individually and figuring out how they apply to our actual lives—practically. How they can help us push back against the pressing of the enemy. Because learning spiritual truths and information without application does not empower us to live a victorious life.

I remember years ago someone introduced me to the concept of spiritual bulimia versus spiritual anorexia as a metaphor. As a disclaimer, I want to make it clear that I am in no way making light of the anorexic or bulimic eating disorders. I'm using them as an illustration to shed light on a spiritual concept. For the sake of this analogy, please follow along with me.

A minister once shared with me that spiritual anorexics are the people who do not take in the Word of God at all. In John 6:35 Jesus replied, "I am the bread of life. Whoever comes to me will never be hungry again. Whoever believes in me will never be thirsty." It stands to reason that anyone not eating their spiritual bread is going to eventually waste way spiritually.

A spiritual bulimic however is someone who gorges on the Word, yet never applies it to their life. Essentially, it's purged and they do not benefit from it. There's no long-term growth. They essentially waste away from spiritual malnutrition as well.

God's Word, His presence, our *relationship* with Him is our bread. Without it we cannot expect to have a healthy, thriving, and strong spiritual life. I have personally known spiritual bulimics. They are always in the Word, they can quote scripture front and back, know where every biblical story is located in the bible and tell you all kinds of facts about the Bible, however their lives show little to zero evidence of its POWER. There's no application and therefore no fruit. I've often asked myself how that is even possible.

Years ago, I was speaking to a friend who was contemplating attending seminary. She told me that when she prayed about it, God's answer surprised her. God essentially told her that the minute she started treating and/or reading the Bible as if it were a mere textbook, He would pull her out of seminary. Say what, now!?

Wow! Did you catch that? You may ask, is it even possible to read the Bible as a textbook? It sure is. I guess it would be like memorizing a cookbook and still not knowing how to cook. With the Bible, you can memorize the content, get familiar with the stories, know all the facts, do a million word studies in Greek and Hebrew, even be fluent in Greek and Hebrew! But are you encountering the Living God while you read? Is He giving you instruction for your life and showing you areas He wants to help you improve in? Are you obeying and walking out what He's telling you to do? Is reading His Word bringing you into the ultimate truth of how loved, cherished, and empowered you are? Are you *applying* those truths to your life in order to walk in victory?

Listen, we aren't to going to get it right all the time. The good news is He isn't looking for perfection. But at the end of the day, reading the Word on a regular basis should produce some change in your heart and produce fruit in your life. There should be a maturing process that's evident. Let's explore how this Helmet can help secure us in this battle!

Reaching deeper into the box, we find the helmet! It seems so ordinary, but the purpose of this piece of metal is to protect the head. As mighty as the brain is, it's extremely vulnerable. A solid blow would be fatal. That's why it's the duty of every mother to harass their kids to wear helmets while riding their bikes, scooter, skateboards, etc. Us moms will always be classified as uncool for pushing helmets, but it is what it is. I give zero apologies to my kid concerning the helmet. His noggin is the most important part of his body and for now I'm responsible for said noggin. He'd argue. I'd win. End of story.

Now while I can reason that the helmet can save a life, I'm curious. Why would Paul call this helmet in our armor of God "The Helmet of Salvation?" Especially when he's talking to believers? Have you ever thought about that? I was recently doing some research on the Helmet of Salvation and was surprised to find that many articles and studies took a sharp turn into Soteriology — the study of the doctrine of salvation. Some believe Christians don't need to wear the Helmet of Salvation because we're already saved. Can I get a side eye emoji? Wasn't Paul talking to Christians when he was unpacking the Armor of God to begin with? I started to write about all these rabbit trails and then told myself … Nope! Not going there today. That topic could literally be a whole 'nother book.

For the sake of time, my beliefs concerning this topic can be summed up in what we find by reading Titus 3:5–8:

> … he saved us, not because of the righteous things we had done, but because of his mercy. He washed away our sins, giving us a new birth and new life through the Holy Spirit. He generously poured out the Spirit upon us through Jesus Christ our Savior. Because of his grace he declared us righteous and gave us confidence that we will inherit eternal life. This is a trustworthy saying, and I want you to insist on these teachings so that all who trust in God will devote themselves to doing good. These teachings are good and beneficial for everyone.

We certainly cannot *earn* our way into heaven. That would make a complete mockery of the sacrifice Jesus made on the cross. Why would He volunteer to be tortured and die for us if we could do it on our own? You know what else would make a complete mockery of His work on the cross? Not appropriating, applying, and living out the new identity He purchased for us once we received our salvation.

So what is salvation? While it may seem obvious, I want to make sure we are all on the same page. Let's look at a couple of scriptures:

John 3:16 says, "For this is how God loved the world: He gave his one and only Son, so that everyone who believes in him will not perish but have eternal life."

John 14:6 tells us, "Jesus told him, 'I am the way, the truth, and the life. No one can come to the Father except through me.'"

So that covers WHO gave it to us, WHERE the gift of salvation came from, and HOW we can attain it. But WHAT is salvation?

The definition of salvation in general is the preservation or deliverance from harm, ruin, or loss. The theological definition according to the Oxford Dictionary is "deliverance from sin and its consequences, believed by Christians to be brought about by faith in Christ."

Now let's make an important distinction here. Salvation is a gift from God through Jesus. So if we are putting on our helmet of salvation, what *exactly* are we putting on? The answer is we are putting on the *hope* of our salvation. Not like, "I'm hope I'm saved!" but as in "the hope my salvation brings." This is not about wondering/hoping we make it to heaven but about grabbing hold of the promises we are certain to see not just at Christ's return but also in this lifetime as we follow Him. Examples of the hope of our salvation include but are not limited to His promises to never leave us or forsake. We can have hope that we will be victorious in our various battles. We can have hope that He sees us and that He is for us and that if we let Him He will use our lives for His glory!

The enemy's objective is to make us question everything about God: His character, what He said, how much He loves us, etc. He even has people questioning their salvation. I have known people over the years who have struggled to settle the fact that they've asked Jesus to be Lord of their life and that it's a done deal.

Could you imagine having a wonderful wedding and reception, celebrating the union between you and the person you love, only to live out your marriage wondering whether the officiant was licensed and if your marriage was legit? Talk about a gray area. Some days you feel married. Some days you don't. I imagine that kind of limbo would leave you feeling unsettled and dealing with all kinds of anxiety. When people ask you, do you tell them you're married? Or do you say you're not sure? This is a matter that needs to be settled so you know how to proceed in life, wouldn't you say?!

Years ago, I had a friend who shared with me about something she was dealing with in her own marriage. Her husband was living with the constant struggle of doubting his salvation. I recently interviewed her about the experience and why her husband struggled and this is what she had to say:

> **Friend**: I'll tell you what I remember. He was constantly saying the prayer of salvation. He was always afraid that he didn't mean it. It's like his view of God was incorrect. At the core, I think he believed that God was a God of judgment only. He would take sticky notes and write out the prayer of salvation and add the date. There were tons of sticky notes all over our mirror. He would say things like, "Maybe I really did it this time." But he would constantly question whether he really meant it. Then he would make a new sticky note and add a new date. It was compulsive.
>
> He was hung up on the idea that he couldn't possibly mean it. He was afraid of God in an unhealthy way. He believed he had to be good enough. He was convicted by his own thoughts. Eventually he completely backslid [relapsed into sin]. It was weird that he was so fixated on not being completely convinced of his salvation. He was afraid that what was in his heart and what he said was not good enough. He thought it was all about performance.
>
> **Me**: It sounds like he never got it settled and the enemy just had him going in circles. How do you think that affected your relationship and your marriage back then?
>
> **Friend**: It destroyed the marriage. We ended up divorced. He ultimately backslid into a lifestyle of sin. We had moved out of

state and he chose to surround himself with friends who were not believers. He didn't have a single friend who was a believer and had no desire to get involved in a church. It didn't happen overnight. It was a slow pulling away from everything because he never had his foundation correct to begin with. He then got sucked into the ways of the world. It's a decade later and he still isn't living for the Lord. Sadly, maybe he really isn't saved. It doesn't seem like it was ever really in his heart. It was about works, and living in fear of God, so he was easily pulled into a lifestyle of sin. It grew and grew until it was revealed he was having an affair. His faith was set up on a rocky foundation. Unfortunately, his whole life was destroyed.

Me: In the marriage when he had those sticky notes and he was putting them all over the place, what frame of mind was he in? Was he always anxious? Did he get angry or depressed?

Friend: He was very depressed and fearful. He would go through cycles of lying in bed and meditating on fear. He'd be overcome with sadness, anxiety, and fear of hell. He was meditating on hell instead of meditating on the Lord and how much God loved him. I would reassure him. I would spend a lot of my time telling him over and over again, "Surely you meant it" [concerning the sinner's prayer].

Back then I didn't have the revelation that I have now. Now I realize I was trying to do something that I can't do: I can't be his Holy Spirit. I couldn't convince him his heart was right. I didn't know his heart. All I knew was he said the prayer and the Bible says if you say it, you're born again, as long as you said it from your heart. Every time I would say that, I could tell it would go in one ear and out the other. His heart was rocky soil, like the parable in the Bible (Matthew 13:3-9). My words were falling on deaf ears because he was so convinced that he wasn't good enough. That whatever he said was not good enough for God. Like he didn't mean it *enough!*

So yes, it was a fixation on fear and he would be depressed. He would become very sad. He was like a person who is clinically depressed, but on one of their bad days. He would lie in bed all day and sulk. He couldn't snap out of it. It was a cycle. He would get very depressed until he was finally able to break out. And I never knew what would break him out of it each time.

Me: I think you identified the tactic of the enemy right there. There was a fixation on hell and a fixation on good works, on being good enough. The full message of the gospel, that salvation is *not* a result of works but a gift you could never earn, wasn't taking root. That foundational truth never went down deep in his heart. He could never earn the ability to enter into heaven. And the enemy completely assaulted the hope of his salvation. He was not able to fully put on his Helmet of Salvation. Unfortunately, it's like it just stayed on the shelf.

The matter of eternity must be settled in your heart! If the enemy can get you to constantly keep questioning your salvation, it will be very difficult for you to do anything fruitful for the kingdom. How can you live out and *put on* the hope of salvation if the salvation part is not resolved. You're stuck doing what my pastor refers to as "navel gazing." That's when a person focuses on themselves and their issues to the point they have no bandwidth to impact others for the kingdom in any way, shape, or form. And bingo, that's where the enemy wants every believer to be – in a prison of their own making, so he doesn't even have to fight them.

Proverbs 23:7 (KJV) says, "For as he thinketh in his heart, so *is* he."

You liked that King James flow right there, didn't you? Had to switch it up on you guys! Back to my boy John Wooden. Well, he's not really my boy per se. I just seem to like a lot of his quotes. He says, "A test of a person's character is what it takes to discourage him." Your mind is a battlefield in and of itself. We've got to put protection in place to maximize our chances for success. Our helmet, our Helmet of Salvation, is our protection.

So how do I put on my Helmet of Salvation? What does that look like practically, you may ask. Let's walk it out. Remember we aren't putting on salvation every day. Meaning we are not asking Jesus to be Lord of our lives in order to get saved every day. Sure, there are seasons where we can recommit our lives after being estranged for some time. That's not what we are focusing on here. We're addressing the daily discipline of putting on the *hope of our salvation.*

If you haven't asked Jesus to be Lord of your life yet, now is as good a time as any. I assure you, Jesus isn't the same as the people who have hurt you, whether they professed Christ or not. I've heard it many times, "You Christians ... ." I want to address those on the fence or those who are dealing with "Church hurt." Let's face it, there are a lot of Christians out there who are not the best representation of Christ. I admit it, I've missed the mark myself on many occasions. I, like many, are still "work[ing] hard to show the results of [my] salvation, obeying God with deep reverence and fear" (Philippians 2:12). It's a process. However, your salvation is your responsibility. It's your personal relationship with Christ. Deciding not to give your life to Christ because of Christians who have failed you is like vowing to never date or get married because you've witnessed too many break ups. Jesus is calling you and wooing you because He's head over heels in love with you. He's sorry so many people failed you and let you down. He's promised to never do that. You can trust Him.

Is that good or is that good!? My thoughts exactly!

CHAPTER 13

Putting on the Helmet of Salvation

*Take the helmet of salvation ... and pray in the Spirit on
all occasions with all kinds of prayers and requests.*
Ephesian 6:16

So, I've already shared with you about my salvation. Remember that whole "thought I was saved but I really wasn't" testimony back in chapter five? Wild, right? My mindset was that since I was in church all the time, since my parents were Christians, and since I was behaving properly (most of the time anyway), that I was a shoo-in to get into heaven. Right? WRONG! Thankfully Papa God was gracious enough to come and course correct me and I've never been the same since.

If you are not 100% certain whether you are just a churchgoer or are saved, I invite you to pause right now and talk to God. After all, He wants a relationship with you!

One of my favorite Christian songs is "I Put On Christ" by Laura Hackett. If I had to pick a theme song for this book (because that's a thing), this song would be in the top three. I encourage you to look it up on YouTube right now. Find the live version if you're not familiar with it. Warning: The song is anointed! Don't be surprised or alarmed if you feel the presence of the Holy Spirit while listening. It's FIRE! Every time I listen I go into "I am Sparta!" mode. It's very helpful when you're knocking out goals or working out, not so much when you're making dinner – gets kind of messy. But I digress. The whole entire song is about the battle we are in as believers and the strategies we implement to win our battles. Many scripture references can be found in the lyrics of the song:

> **Romans 13:14** - "Instead, clothe yourself with the presence of the Lord Jesus Christ. And don't let yourself think about ways to indulge your evil desires."

> **1 Corinthians 9:26 (NASB)** – "Therefore I run in such a way, as not without aim; I box in such a way, as not beating the air … ."

> **Psalm 144:1** – "Praise the LORD, who is my rock. He trains my hands for war and gives my fingers skill for battle."

Did I mention I love songs that quote scripture? It really helps those truths go down deep in my spirit. Plus, it's easier for me to memorize song lyrics, as a singer/musician, than trying to memorize scripture alone. I'm seriously getting so hype just typing about this song! I may have listened to it 100 times while writing this chapter.

You see, I'm not your typical girl. While I love to dress cute and accessorize, I'm all about a good battle! Give me all the action! Give me all the James Bond espionage-type movies. Give me all the historical dramas about the battles in the Joseon era and other Korean dynasties. I love excursions where I get muddy and filthy, off-roading in four wheelers. I'm adventurous and work well under pressure. I love to see people fighting for justice and what they believe in and if said battle comes with some amazing costumes, even better! Blame my thespian heart.

This song reminds me that we're involved in the most epic battle of all time! Light versus darkness! The Holy God, Creator of the universe, against the schemes of darkness. We are part of this fight and we've got to get our heads in the game. Some of you went there and started singing that "Get'cha Head in the Game" song from *High School Musical*. Admit it!

We have to put on our Helmet of Salvation. The hope of our salvation and everything we receive from salvation. I love how Joyce Meyers said it in one of her sermons: "Think like somebody saved! Have a confident expectation that something good is going to happen to you!" Yes! The hope of your salvation is:

- Knowing your future is secure in Christ!
- Knowing you've been redeemed from death!
- Knowing that there's a purpose and plan for your life!
- Knowing that you are an important part of advancing the kingdom of God!
- Knowing that if God is for you, it doesn't matter who is against you!
- Knowing you can do all things through Christ who gives you strength!
- Knowing your hope is built on nothing less than Jesus' blood and righteousness!

Many years ago, while I was still attending the church I got saved in, the Lord started doing a new thing in my heart and spirit. Ever since I was a kid, I would have very detailed dreams. I had very vivid dreams and moreover they were prophetic dreams. I would tell my parents about my dreams and, since they were both dreamers themselves, I could tell they discerned that sometimes my dreams were significant ... except that one time.

When I was in early elementary school, I remember having a dream about one of my mom's friends. She was an older woman who had never been married and never had any kids. I had a dream that this woman had gotten married. So I shared that with my parents at the breakfast table the next morning. There was silence, followed by raucous laughter. Everyone assumed she'd be single forever. Not even two weeks later she told my parents she had met someone and a couple of months later she was married. BOOM!

I've had those kinds of dreams as far back as I can remember. So back in 2003, when these dreams started increasing in quantity and intensity, I knew I needed some guidance. That journey to find help led me into the exciting world of all things Holy Spirit and the prophetic (hearing the voice and heart of God). Many Christians believe God communicates with us via subtle signs like highlighting pertinent scripture for our current situation. However, in the earlier 2000s, God began to open my eyes to the fact the He communicates intentionally and directly in this very day and age; many times through prophetic words from other believers. The very first prophetic word I remember recording/writing down was from 2004. I literally have a Word document of prophetic words dating all the way back to then.

I have to say, over the years my prophetic words have been a very key part of putting on my Helmet of Salvation. Prophetic words are pretty much small snapshots of things to hope for in your salvation, are they not? I believe many prophetic words are conditional and require us to agree, align, and war over them to bring them to completion. Some prophetic words are absolute, but many are God's invitation to *partner* with Him for something bigger than we could ever accomplish on our own. That's the Hope of our Salvation.

Every day we need to put on our Helmet of Salvation, our hope, believing God will complete the good work He has begun in us. Believing that our latter will be greater than our former. Believing the battle is the Lord's and we've already won. The enemy will attempt to throw you off with all kinds of mind games like:

- Am I really saved?
- Can God really use me?
- Does He even see me? Love me?
- I've sinned too much to be used by God.
- My past is way too complicated.
- Did that last sin make me lose my salvation?

May I remind you again of I Peter 1:13 (KJV): "Wherefore gird up the loins of your mind, be sober, and hope to the end for the grace that is to be brought unto you at the revelation of Jesus Christ ... ."

My friends, put on the mind of Christ! Study what He has to say about you and your situation. Recite it. Declare it and decree it until your mind comes into alignment with His truth. Post it all over your house until you really get it and believe it.

I read my prophetic words over and over and over again. Sometimes I'm stunned when I see the same themes and truths being expressed. I have these moments when I think, "Wow! He must really mean that!? He has sent multiple people over the course of many years and from many different circles to give me the same message! I need to stop doubting this. I need to come into alignment with this. This is His hope for my salvation and I need to partner with Him to make sure it comes to pass!"

But don't take my word for it. Let's do an activation!

I want you to get someplace quiet and grab a pen and paper. I want you to ask God, "What is the hope of my salvation?" And there's no need to overcomplicate this.

- What is the first word or picture that came to mind?
- Did He remind you of a prophetic word that someone gave you?
- Did you immediately think of a dream you had a long time ago?
- Did He show you an area of your life that keeps coming under attack over and over again? (Because the enemy tends to overplay his hand and, in the process, he actually highlights your destiny.)
- Did God highlight a particular scripture?

Whatever He showed you, grab hold of it! Partner with Him to see it to completion. Let it be activated in your life today! Rest in His promises.

No one and nothing can snatch you from God's hands. That's the hope of your salvation right there. Rest assured in it! Come into agreement with it. Put on the mind of Christ. Helmets on, my friends! He has work for you to do!

CHAPTER 14

Sword of the Spirit

here's a passage in Hebrews that says, "For the word of God is alive and powerful. It is sharper than the sharpest two-edged sword, cutting between soul and spirit, between joint and marrow. It exposes our innermost thoughts and desires." (Hebrews 4:12)

Another translation of the same verse says, "For the word of God is living and active" (NASB).

I'm going to let you marinate on that one for a minute.

.

.

.

.

.

Now read it again.

.

.

.

.

I never stop being fascinated by the fact that in the *entire* inventory of spiritual armor, we only have one offensive weapon. Let's review.

- The Belt of Truth - *defense.*
- The Breastplate of Righteousness – *defense.*
- The Gospel Shoes – *defense.*
- The Helmet of Salvation – *defense.*
- The Shield of Faith … now I know Captain America nailed some killer stunts and took out tons of enemies by chucking his shield, but let's get back to the Roman soldiers. The shield was *DEFENSE.*

Our only offensive weapon is the Sword of the Spirit. *WHICH. IS. THE. WORD. OF. GOD.* Our only offensive weaponry is God's Word. Is anyone else just floored by that other than me?

Listen, we can dig our heels in against the enemy with our Gospel Shoes on (so he can't push us back). We can stop fiery darts with our Shield of Faith. We can stay unwavering in the hope of our Helmet of Salvation. We can get girded up with our Belt of Truth which keeps all the armor in place. BUT … would you step into battle with nothing but protective gear on?

I'm about to digress … again.

The other day I was watching my son play a video game online with friends. The more I watched, the more questions I had. One of his "enemies" walked right past the building he was inside of. My son was hidden and they didn't see him. However, they literally walked right in front of him … and he did nothing.

In the next scene I see him run a few feet then duck behind a shed. Then he runs a few more feet and hides behind a massive tree. Then he runs again and crouches behind an overturned vehicle. I'm baffled as, once again, another one of his enemies passes by him and he lets them live!

Now I've already confessed my love for a good battle, so this just wasn't sitting well with me. Finally, I asked him why in the world he was allowing all his enemies to cross his path without ending them! He just very calmly states, "Oh. It's because I don't have a gun or any other weapons." I busted out laughing! He was essentially playing, in my opinion, a game of hide and seek. He was not confident enough to engage in battle because he had no offensive weapons. That'll preach!

If I'm going into war, I want to have *something* in my hands! I don't even care what it is. Call me a Neanderthal and give me a club. Give me Katniss Everdeen's bow and arrow. Give me a gun … well, maybe not. My last experience at a shooting range ended when a hot shell popped backwards and fell down the front of my shirt. Yeah. Still working through that trauma. Give me David's slingshot and a few rocks. Give me Thor's hammer or … wait … did we ever figure out why Captain America was able to pick that thing up in the Endgame movie? I still have questions … lots of questions. But I digress. AGAIN.

Most people would want some kind of weapon, offensive weapon, to fight against their enemy. It just makes sense. So, of course, our loving Father wouldn't leave us without one. After all, He's more passionate about us being victorious than we are. He's not going to load us up with useless items either. Scripture tells us that the Word of God is *ALIVE, ACTIVE, LIVING, BREATHING and POWERFUL!* I'm just in awe. We're fighting with His words. It's times like this that I'm reminded of the following verses:

> **Isaiah 55:9** - "For just as the heavens are higher than the earth, so my ways are higher than your ways and my thoughts higher than your thoughts."

> **1 Corinthians 1:27** – "But God has chosen the foolish things of the world to confound the wise; and God has chosen the weak things of the world to confound the things which are mighty."

> **Job 36:26 (KJV)** - "Behold God is Great and we do not know Him!" or the NLT says it this way, "Look, God is greater than we can understand." My girl Dana Russell wrote a song about just that called "Behold God is Great." Check it out!

I think it's funny how we grew up singing, "Sticks and stones will break my bones but words will never hurt me." Insert side eye emoji. Flash back to the beginning of time. Genesis 1:1-5 says,

> In the beginning God created the heavens and the earth. The earth was formless and empty, and darkness covered the deep waters. And the Spirit of God was hovering over the surface of the waters. Then God *said*, "Let there be light," and there was light. And God saw that the light was good. Then he separated the light from the darkness. God called the light "day" and the darkness "night."

Yeah … the power of words. His are ALIVE, ACTIVE, LIVING, BREATHING and POWERFUL! I'm never going to get tired of saying that, by the way. And because He made us in His likeness, He blessed our words with power as well.

Even though I'm no longer part of the Southern Baptist church where I originally got saved, I am so grateful my journey started there. I've had the opportunity to be part of many churches and many denominations. While other people have used denominational differences to stir up strife and throw shade, I take great joy in expressing the different jewels I've uncovered and gleaned from each season with each one. I won't cover them all here, but I will say that from the Southern Baptists I took with me the deep reverence and *love* of the Word of God. The desire to honor it and cherish it like it should be. The deeper our reverence for God and our relationship with Him grows, the more we naturally cherish His words as well. Reading our Bibles, in my opinion, feels like sitting at His feet and letting Him talk to us.

Early in my spiritual walk as a teenager, my quiet times or "sitting at His feet" times were comprised of age-appropriate devotionals. I loved picking a topic that I felt the Lord was highlighting in my life. Then I'd run to the Christian bookstore to find a devotional that would specifically address the selected topic. It fed the Type A part of my personality. I liked the structure and not having to select what to read each day.

Also me: When I didn't have a particular study I was working through, it was sometimes like a game of Russian Roulette. I would flip my Bible open and then point. Let the reading begin! LOL! Listen, don't knock it. I've had some *amazingly* powerful times with the Lord using that method. And I'd be lying if I said I haven't used this method in my adult years. Look here,

Holy Spirit is powerful enough to land you exactly where He wants you! Don't get it twisted!

Knowing what the Word of God says is vital to our victory! You could say it's our clap back to the enemy when he tries to instill fear or tries to steal from us. However, even the phrase *clap back* is so, so weak and inadequate in describing just how powerful God's Word is. When we decree the Word of God, things happen. Atmospheres shifts! Demons are scattered! Blind eyes are opened! Chains are broken! The future changes! Destinies are released! Prodigals come home! Wombs are opened! The lonely are placed in families! Debts are cancelled! Resources multiply! Fear dissipates! Promotions are actualized! Blessings being held up are released! And that's just a few examples.

Spiritual warfare is as simple and powerful as taking hold of a biblical truth and declaring it and decreeing it over your situation. Your doctor gives you a diagnosis? "Siri, pull up all the scriptures about healing." And you know what's even better than Siri pulling up all the healing-related scriptures? Already having them ingrained in your spirit from reading about them daily.

Proverbs 18:21 says, "Life and death are in the power of the tongue." So, what are you going to speak over your life? You may think that's a dumb question, but I hear people saying things like, "I'm dead!" after a funny joke. I hear people saying, "I'm sick and tired of ... ." I hear people say, "Well my mom and grandmother had XYZ so I probably will too." Really? You're just going to let that be the final verdict? Please hear my heart! That's not judgment or condemnation at all. That's me saying we may want to speak a better word over our lives and situations! I'm rooting for you to change the narrative in your own life! I'm rooting for you to change the narrative for your bloodline! Leave them a POWERFUL legacy!

Several months ago I overheard my son say, "I suck at this game!" after losing a video game battle. My response? "Keep on saying that and you may continue to." He stared at me for the longest time, processing. I said, "What!? You're the one who gave the enemy the rest of the day off because you chose to take over his job for him. The second you take his lies and start speaking them over yourself, his job is done!" The next time he lost a game I heard him say from the other room, "I'm *so* gonna get better at this game." Well done, son, well done!

This truth is so important, especially when we're in the middle of the battle. Emotions are running high. We're sometimes battle weary. But guess what? If you don't quit, you win! Get those scriptures down in your heart. I am not the best when it comes to memorizing scripture, but I am a visual learner. If I keep seeing a verse, I eventually start paraphrasing it, then quoting it verbatim, and then, lo and behold, I start even quoting the reference (book/chapter/verse).

In Deuteronomy 6:9 it says, "Write them on the doorposts of your house and on your gates." I say also write them on the mirrors in your bathroom. Post them on index cards on your fridge. Put them in picture frames around your house. Whatever methods work for you, do them and do them diligently. Also, keep in mind that different seasons will call for different strategies, so don't feel boxed in with any particular method. Just flow with Holy Spirit, your Helper.

For those of you who are more visual, you might imagine that every time you quote a scripture in the heat of the battle, it's like punching the enemy in the gut! Imagine that whenever you quote a healing scripture, your physical body gets stronger. Or every time you declare and decree over your prodigal, they take one step closer to home. Or every time you speak His Word over situations you feel caged in by, one more prison bar snaps in half.

His words have power and deal deadly blows to the enemy. His words in your mouth have power, too! So use your sword! Don't be the warrior in the middle of the battle hiding behind trees and walls. Stand up! Come out in the open! Take your authority! Wield your power! You were made for this!

CHAPTER 15

Wielding the Sword of the Spirit

Take the sword of the Spirit, which is the word of God.
Ephesians 6:17b

*L*et's talk about gifts and callings for a minute ... or ten. When we align with Christ and make him Lord of our lives, we draw a distinct line in the sand and the enemy doesn't like it. Many new believers experience the shift and the warfare after they get saved. The enemy also amps up his tactics when we start to walk in our destiny and calling. You may wonder what a "calling" is. A while back we talked about being fearfully and wonderfully made. To get even more specific, when God created you, He created you with a very specific purpose in mind. If the enemy can't keep you from aligning with Christ, he'll definitely try to prevent you from fulfilling your purpose, destiny, and/or calling.

Some of you know what you are called to do on this earth. You may not have all the details, but you have the general gist. Especially if you're in a prophetic circle, you may have heard the same calling prophesied over you a few times. I have a friend that always says, "God and I operate on a need-to-know basis. If He hasn't told me, it's because apparently I don't need to know." Haha! I aspire to be at such a place of peace in the midst of waiting. Most of the time the details of our calling are revealed as we follow the breadcrumbs God gives us on our path.

Here's an example. Back in April 2020, as I sat on my bed talking to the Lord, He suggested I start "doing videos." I was perplexed. He explained to me that many of the people I mentor and coach come to me with similar questions. He said I should make videos to encourage people in their walk and I could always refer folks back to certain video topics in the future. It made sense to me. I immediately got off the bed and announced on my Instagram page that I'd be doing videos. The response was overwhelming. Some people were saying, "It's about time!" Others were telling me they were going to send their friends and family my way. Overall, folks were really excited, which I was not expecting at all.

Long story short, I decided to create a new public Instagram page under my name, as well as a YouTube channel, to accommodate the new followers. Both of those pages have opened up so many doors! Invitations to speak at women's conferences, to lead worship, to do tv interviews talking about the prophetic ministries I'm involved in at my church, and the book I was writing. The many opportunities it has provided me to minister to random strangers is amazing. Then six months later, the Lord officially called me into ministry.

At this point, I still don't have a full understanding of what this ministry will entail. However, what I do know is that my obedience leads to promotion and greater responsibility, and then He releases more breadcrumbs and more details. It's like a scavenger hunt sometimes. As we follow and obey, we get more clues and we come into the fullness of the purpose He intended for us!

However, there are times on the journey when the weight of God's calling can feel like it's going to completely crush you. The pressure, at times, is simply too intense to articulate. I'm sure, without knowing them personally, that King David, Apostle Paul, and Job could attest to that. All three of these men were called to walk through something they never asked to be a part of.

David was minding his own business in the field tending to his flock when Prophet Samuel came to his town to anoint him as king. Here's the story in 1 Samuel 16:6–13:

When they arrived, Samuel took one look at Eliab and thought, "Surely this is the Lord's anointed!"

But the Lord said to Samuel, "Don't judge by his appearance or height, for I have rejected him. The Lord doesn't see things the way you see them. People judge by outward appearance, but the Lord looks at the heart."

Then Jesse told his son Abinadab to step forward and walk in front of Samuel. But Samuel said, "This is not the one the Lord has chosen." Next Jesse summoned Shimea, but Samuel said, "Neither is this the one the Lord has chosen." In the same way all seven of Jesse's sons were presented to Samuel. But Samuel said to Jesse, "The Lord has not chosen any of these." Then Samuel asked, "Are these all the sons you have?"

"There is still the youngest," Jesse replied. "But he's out in the fields watching the sheep and goats."

"Send for him at once," Samuel said. "We will not sit down to eat until he arrives."

So Jesse sent for him. He was dark and handsome, with beautiful eyes.

And the Lord said, "This is the one; anoint him."

So as David stood there among his brothers, Samuel took the flask of olive oil he had brought and anointed David with the oil. And the Spirit of the Lord came powerfully upon David from that day on.

To add insult to injury, his entire family attended this meeting specifically because the Prophet was coming ... and David wasn't even invited to the gathering! But God! The next thing we see is the "black sheep" shepherd now being anointed as the next king … of the entire nation! How many black sheep of the family do I have out there reading this? I'm raising my hand with you. You can relate to David far better than most. Be encouraged. God chooses the least likely and sees those that others choose to ignore and brush aside. When God chooses you and singles you out, what will you do? Will you accept His call?

Saul from the New Testament (who then became Paul) was minding his own business walking down a road to Damascus when he was struck blind and given his calling. Can you imagine? This part of his story is in Acts 9:1-19:

> Meanwhile, Saul was uttering threats with every breath and was eager to kill the Lord's followers. So he went to the high priest. He requested letters addressed to the synagogues in Damascus, asking for their cooperation in the arrest of any followers of the Way he found there. He wanted to bring them—both men and women—back to Jerusalem in chains.

> As he was approaching Damascus on this mission, a light from heaven suddenly shone down around him. He fell to the ground and heard a voice saying to him, "Saul! Saul! Why are you persecuting me?"

> "Who are you, lord?" Saul asked.

> And the voice replied, "I am Jesus, the one you are persecuting! Now get up and go into the city, and you will be told what you must do."

> The men with Saul stood speechless, for they heard the sound of someone's voice but saw no one! Saul picked himself up off the ground, but when he opened his eyes he was blind. So his companions led him by the hand to Damascus. ⁹ He remained there blind for three days and did not eat or drink.

Now there was a believer in Damascus named Ananias. The Lord spoke to him in a vision, calling, "Ananias!"

"Yes, Lord!" he replied.

The Lord said, "Go over to Straight Street, to the house of Judas. When you get there, ask for a man from Tarsus named Saul. He is praying to me right now. I have shown him a vision of a man named Ananias coming in and laying hands on him so he can see again."

"But Lord," exclaimed Ananias, "I've heard many people talk about the terrible things this man has done to the believers in Jerusalem! And he is authorized by the leading priests to arrest everyone who calls upon your name."

But the Lord said, "Go, for Saul is my chosen instrument to take my message to the Gentiles and to kings, as well as to the people of Israel. And I will show him how much he must suffer for my name's sake."

So Ananias went and found Saul. He laid his hands on him and said, "Brother Saul, the Lord Jesus, who appeared to you on the road, has sent me so that you might regain your sight and be filled with the Holy Spirit." Instantly something like scales fell from Saul's eyes, and he regained his sight. Then he got up and was baptized. Afterward he ate some food and regained his strength."

Saul had spent his career persecuting and murdering Christians and now he was being tasked with being an Apostle to the very Christians he'd been persecuting the day before. Can you imagine the reception he received when he went to preach his first sermon? It probably looked something like roaches scattering when the light came on. Maybe it's just me, but I wonder how many "speaking engagements" it took before he started gaining the believers' trust. Talk about feeling like you're set up to fail, right?!

Job was minding his own business bringing sacrifices to God on behalf of all his children when he received bad news, after bad news, after bad news. The first wave of bad news was enough to kill someone … but somehow he endured many crashing waves that day. This part of his story is in Job 1:13–22:

> One day when Job's sons and daughters were feasting at the oldest brother's house, a messenger arrived at Job's home with this news: "Your oxen were plowing, with the donkeys feeding beside them, when the Sabeans raided us. They stole all the animals and killed all the farmhands. I am the only one who escaped to tell you."

> While he was still speaking, another messenger arrived with this news: "The fire of God has fallen from heaven and burned up your sheep and all the shepherds. I am the only one who escaped to tell you."

> While he was still speaking, a third messenger arrived with this news: "Three bands of Chaldean raiders have stolen your camels and killed your servants. I am the only one who escaped to tell you."

> While he was still speaking, another messenger arrived with this news: "Your sons and daughters were feasting in their oldest brother's home. Suddenly, a powerful wind swept in from the wilderness and hit the house on all sides. The house collapsed, and all your children are dead. I am the only one who escaped to tell you."

> Job stood up and tore his robe in grief. Then he shaved his head and fell to the ground to worship. He said,

"I came naked from my mother's womb,
and I will be naked when I leave.
The Lord gave me what I had,
and the Lord has taken it away.
Praise the name of the Lord!"

In all of this, Job did not sin by blaming God.

Now Job was a man who walked uprightly before the Lord. Job 1:1b says, "He was blameless—a man of complete integrity. He feared God and stayed away from evil." Yet he was facing many trials that someone of his character should never see based on the belief systems of his day and age. If his grief wasn't enough, he also had to endure friends who accused him of being evil … the very ones who should have been comforting him. His wife's advice was to "curse God and die." (Job 2:9b) Oh the weight of what he had to endure. The many questions that must have tortured him.

These men have three very distinctly different stories. However, one thing they all had in common is they each had to endure a severe amount of pressing. Let's look a little deeper at David and how he endured his pressing.

David goes on to live a life on the run from the very man he's trying to serve, King Saul. He was literally running for his life. The root of Saul's issues with David was jealousy. Saul eventually became David's father in-law, after David killed Goliath and saved the entire nation of Israel. I sense the jealousy started after David killed Goliath, because the Bible says the women were singing in the streets, "Saul has killed his thousands, and David his ten thousands!" (I Samuel 18:7). Then the Bible tells us, "This made Saul very angry. 'What's this?' he said. 'They credit David with ten thousands and me with only thousands. Next they'll be making him their king!'" (1 Samuel 18:7-8).

Did I mention that David and Jonathan, Saul's son, were BFFs? I mean this plot is juicer than most TV shows! Not even playing around! The amount of injustice and rejection David suffered at the hand of Saul is unbelievable. The story of how David continues to honor Saul in the midst of demonic persecution is one for the books! Not this particular book, haha! But the book of Samuel, in the Bible, is chock full of flesh singe-ing principles that I may tackle in the future. But for now, back to his pressing.

So how did David endure?

Pick a Psalm, any Psalm! LOL! Just kidding. Not all of the Psalms were written by David. And of the ones that were written by him, only a portion were penned during this particular season of his life. Let's take a look at one of them. I'll start with Psalm 59. One of my favorite things about David and his Psalms is that there's no pussyfooting around his intense and challenging emotions. He fully acknowledges where he is mentally and emotionally. He speaks his truth to God because he's obviously secure, not only about who he is, but also about their relationship and the nature of the God he serves. I find that aspect of David so refreshing and inviting. He wasn't nicknamed the "Man After God's Own Heart" for no reason.

Here are a few quotes from David's Psalm 59, written when Saul sent soldiers to watch David's house in order to kill him:

Verse 1: "Rescue me from my enemies, Oh God. Protect me from those who come to destroy me!"

Verse 4: "I have done nothing wrong, yet they prepare to attack me. Wake up! See what's happening to me!"

Have you ever been this real with God? Did you realize you can be? I mean ... the cat's already out of the bag. Psalms 139:2 says, "You know when I sit down or stand up. You know my thoughts even when I'm far away."

Yup ... cat's *been* out of the bag! He already knows what you're thinking.

Verse 5: "Oh Lord God of Heaven's Armies, the God of Israel ... ."

Verses 9-10: "You are my strength; I wait for you to rescue me, for You, O God, are my fortress. In his unfailing love, my God will stand with me."

David comes to God bare and completely vulnerable. He's not putting on any airs or trying to pray eloquent prayers. He boldly comes to the throne to have a conversation with His Creator. There's an open invitation for all of us to do the same. You know they say God doesn't have favorites, although secretly I think it's me. LOL. He's just trying not to hurt all of your feelings. ;)

When the weight of your calling or the weight of the season you're in feels like it's going to crush you, run to your Strong Tower. It's in Him you will be strengthened. He says, "My power works best in weakness" (2 Corinthians 12:9). You don't have to come to him with eloquent words. I can remember one particular season in my life that I would come to Him and just weep and weep and weep until I couldn't weep anymore. I once heard someone say that God counts even our tears as prayer and intercession.

Psalm 56:8 says, "You keep track of all my sorrows. You have collected all my tears in your bottle. You have recorded each one in your book."

During that particular season in life, I would constantly get prophetic words quoting Psalm 126:5 (NASB): "Those who sow in tears shall reap with joyful shouting." If I'm honest, I got to the point where I was on the verge of despising that verse. Then Holy Spirit gave me revelation and I turned it into my weapon!

I began declaring, "YES GOD! I have been sowing in tears for many, many years and I WILL reap with joyful shouting!"

In 2019, I finally came through and out of *the most* brutally pressing season of my entire life. I have never been pressed so hard by the enemy, and I've never had to press into my Maker more than I had to over the past 10+ years. It was dark. It was lonely. I felt like my heart was literally breaking over and over again. I experienced betrayal after betrayal on a level I never had before. Like I mentioned earlier, I cried more in that season than I have the rest of my life combined. I got a PhD in forgiving 70 X 7 times, like Jesus spoke of in Matthew 18.

My weapon all along the way was God's written word and the prophetic words He sent people to speak over my life. I will never be able to fully express my gratitude to and for all those who spoke life over me during my valley of weeping. There were times it seemed I was just swinging my Sword aimlessly. I declared and decreed scripture just to speak it – just in case a foe was approaching, because there were moments I was too weary and too down to even look up.

That brings me to another "secret" weapon we're given that's revealed at the end of Ephesian 6:16, "and pray in the Spirit on all occasions with all kinds of prayers and requests." If spiritual warfare was a game show, praying in the spirit would definitely be the "phone a friend" option! Do you mean to tell me that when I'm downright spent and do not even have the energy to look up scripture and declare them, I can just tag in Holy Spirit and He'll take over for me? Say whaaaaaaaaaat, now?! Just picture me as the next "The Price is Right" contestant running down the aisle, cause I'm going to step right up for that offer!

The gift of tongues is one of the evidences of being baptized in the Holy Spirit, as explained in Acts 2. The wonderful thing is, when we don't know how to pray, we can pray in the Spirit. Romans 8:26 says, "And the Holy Spirit helps us in our weakness. For example, we don't know what God wants us to pray for. But the Holy Spirit prays for us with groanings that cannot be expressed in words." Who can offer a better and more powerful prayer than the one Holy Spirit prays on your behalf? I'm waiting ... right? Case closed.

I'm so grateful to God for all these tools He gives us to overcome our enemy. Guys ... God is so intentional and so strategic. He does not waste any word or action. His plans are perfectly mapped out and executed. These individual items within the Armor of God are undefeatable when we use them as He intends us to. We have been set up to win! I'm so grateful that He tells us we are more than conquerors. So thankful for Him sending us a Helper, Holy Spirit. If you thought your chances were bleak when you started reading this book, I pray you've been convinced otherwise. No matter what the enemy sends your way God is not shocked and He already has a plan to execute your victory.

Now that you know all about the armor and weapons God has made available for you to use when the enemy attacks you, let's talk about what those attacks might look like practically.

CHAPTER 16

When We're Pressed by Rejection

I n this and the following chapter, I want to expose some of the common tactics of the enemy. We touched on a few as we explored our armor, but the ones I'm sharing now are the ones the enemy has used to press me personally. And the main one he's used on me is rejection. You may be able to relate.

I now believe that rejection is a blessing in disguise. If you had said that to me 20 years ago, I probably would have grabbed my purse, stood up, and walked out ... like that gif with Viola Davis! It's one of my personal favorites.

In my life, I have experienced all kinds of rejection. Rejection from family, friends, a former spouse, bosses, church leaders ... you name it. To say God walked me through some very challenging circumstances would be putting it mildly. During one year, the Lord did a very deep work of healing in my heart and, in the process, He referred me back to the story of Leah. Do you guys remember Leah in the Bible? Shall we take a walk down memory lane – or should I say, Old Testament lane?

Leah's story can be found in Genesis chapters 29-35. Leah and her younger sister Rachel were both married to Jacob. In this dramatic saga that would put most Lifetime Made-For-Television-Movies to shame, we find a trickster (Jacob) who meets his match in his soon to be father-in-law (Laban). Here comes the NCV (New Cassandra Version) again:

Jacob sees Rachel and falls hard for her. He approaches Laban, her father, and asks for her hand in marriage. Laban, who is a shady opportunist, strikes up a deal with Jacob. He offers Jacob his daughter's hand in marriage if Jacob will work for him for seven years. Jacob is so sprung that seven years is a drop in a bucket as far as he's concerned. He takes the offer and works for Laban for seven years. Wedding day comes around, he marries his bride and beds her, only to find out the next morning – *surprise* – it's not Rachel he married, but Leah, her older sister.

Jacob confronts Laban, and Laban's response is literally that it's not customary to marry off the younger sister before the older sister... Are you hearing the crickets, too? Seriously, Laban? You didn't think to mention this a wee bit earlier? Wow! I believe Laban purposely scammed Jacob. But Jacob was unrelenting. He immediately strikes up another deal with Laban to marry Rachel and they agree on another seven years! Jacob deeply loved Rachel. It's very, very romantic.

What about Leah, though? Can you imagine how she must have felt? Her dad was simply using her as a pawn to trick Jacob. She was caught in the middle of his dishonest plot. I'm sure she felt *pressed* on every side. What did that do to her relationship with her sister? The Bible makes it very clear that Rachel was the pretty one. Rachel was the one who had Jacob's affection. The first thing Jacob did, after their wedding night, once he realized he was tricked, was run to Laban. Jacob only really cared about winning Rachel. Leah must have felt a ridiculous amount of rejection. She knew she wasn't Jacob's first choice and that she was just a consolation prize. I mean, a week after Jacob married her, he married her sister! Leah must have felt:

- 2nd best
- 2nd class citizen
- Unloved
- Not pretty enough
- A pawn in a game
- Used by the people around her

So how does Leah decide to deal with all this? She starts competing and trying to *prove* her worth. Her sister Rachel was barren, so she hoped the children she produced for Jacob would win his affection. In the midst of her pain, God blessed her with many children. As a matter of fact, it's Leah and not Rachel who we find mentioned in the lineage of Christ. That is doper than dope!

The Lord highlighted her story for me during one of the lowest points I'd ever experienced in my life. I was doing my best to recover from the worst betrayal/rejection of my own, yet I was fumbling. Sure, I had read Leah's story before. But this time I knew God was saying, "You're at a crossroads, daughter. I'm inviting you to a place of healing and restoration from this deep blow of rejection you've experienced. Or you'll live like Leah did and spend the rest of your life trying to prove your worth to people who are never going to value you like you were meant to be valued." His words resonated in the deepest part of my soul. I wept for hours.

I made a choice that weekend. I absolutely *was not* going to spend my life trying to prove anything to anybody. I did the deep work of getting deliverance. I did the work to get inner healing to work on my wounds. I began tearing down the walls I had built up trying to protect myself … they had failed me miserably, by the way. Brick by brick I tore down all the lies that told me that my heavenly Father couldn't protect me, that told me I wasn't enough, that told me I was too much, that told me I needed to tone down who I was in order to accommodate other people's weaknesses and insecurities, that told me I needed to maintain unhealthy boundaries to cater to toxic people. NO MORE! I handed all that garbage to God and He began to restore my soul.

I wish I could tell you it was a quick process, but it wasn't. However, I was okay with that. I wanted this renovation to be done right, so I followed God's lead. He was the one who pointed out to me that rejection was a blessing in disguise. Rejection helps you pinpoint the people who are not for you. Rejection became a weeding out process for me.

Now when I apply for a job and don't get it, I feel a bit of relief, as bizarre as that sounds. I always pray that God will open doors no man can shut and shut doors no man can open (Revelation 3:7). This is one of the ways He highlights His will for my life. Even in friendships! I cannot tell you how many times I meet people and think, "Wow, I should connect with them. They seem like a great person." Then I experience rejection from them and later on God reveals what He protected me from. I don't question rejection anymore. I roll with it. It's a blessing in disguise. I'm a firm believer that what's for me is for me. I am more than willing to back off and allow God to bring me divine connections and divine opportunities. There is grace and favor behind the doors He opens for us versus the ones we try to barrel through and force open.

However, if we cannot press into God and bring our hearts and minds into alignment with what He is doing, rejection will seem like it's crushing our very soul. God has a better way, friends. He wants to heal our hurts, hearts, wounds, and soul. His hope for us can be found in 3 John 1:2. What He wants is for us to prosper, even as our soul prospers. I highly recommend teachings from Katie Souza to understand how the condition of our soul affects so many areas of our life.

Rejection is not your portion. A big part of pushing past rejection is the internal work it takes to be convinced you are who God says you are. When I think about rejection and identity, I also think about the fairytale story of Anastasia.

It's about a royal family, the Romanovs. An evil wizard puts a curse on the family and in the process Anastasia is uprooted from the palace. Sometime later when a reward is announced for the return of Anastasia, a couple of Russians plot to find a random child to pose as the long-lost princess in order to claim the reward money. They choose Anastasia, who at the time is an orphan, because of her "remarkable resemblance" to the actual princess, not knowing they've actually found her!

She was royalty the entire time, but she was living as an orphan. Can you imagine the treatment she received and the level of rejection she felt? Did any of those circumstances change who she really was? Absolutely not! At the appointed time, she was restored to her rightful place. God wants to restore each one of us to our rightful place in this season!

We are royalty. First Peter 2:9 says, "… for you are a chosen people. You are a royal priesthood, a holy nation, God's very own possession. As a result, you can show others the goodness of God, for he called you out of the darkness into his wonderful light." It doesn't matter how others treat us. Our past doesn't matter. Our experiences don't matter. We are sons and daughter of the Most High God.

Have you noticed that God has invited us into His family in every way you can join a family in the natural?

Birth – You can be born into a family, right? Well, John 3:3 says, "Jesus replied, 'I tell you the truth, unless you are born again, you cannot see the Kingdom of God.'"

Marriage – You can be married into a family, right? Well, 2 Corinthians 11:2 tells us, "For I am jealous for you with the jealousy of God himself. I promised you as a pure bride to one husband—Christ." As the Church, Jesus is our Bridegroom.

Adoption – You can be adopted into a family, right? Well, Ephesians 1:5 reminds us, "God decided in advance to adopt us into his own family by bringing us to himself through Jesus Christ. This is what he wanted to do, and it gave him great pleasure." That one right there gets me every time! Did you catch that? This is what He wanted to do! His desire is for you. He sees you and loves you. It gave Him great pleasure. He delights in you. *This* is who you are. *This* is your identity. *This* is your value.

What else does He have to do to prove it to you? He loves you and has done everything to prove His love. Let's take Him at His word. Let's remember who we are and whose we are!

CHAPTER 17

Other Ways We Are Pressed

E arlier this year, the Lord brought to mind someone I knew in the past. I was reminiscing about a time when this person was on fire for the Lord. They were pursuing God and all the things God was calling them to with their whole heart. Fast forward. Many years later we were no longer in contact with one another and rarely spoke. If I'm honest, I didn't even recognize this person anymore when I saw them. This person literally looked different—physically—and the truth was we had nothing in common and nothing to talk about anymore. I felt like they had taken a turn for the worst. I remember asking the Lord, "What happened to them?" This was His response to me:

> **_Complacency_**_! Please don't think that remaining in a stagnant, complacent place is equivalent to staying steady or holding ground. It's actually moving backwards. If everything around you is progressing and you stay in the same place, you are losing ground. Study the concept of complacency and see how it led to the demise of your friend's character._

Whoa! I sat there stunned. I'm still unpacking what He spoke to me months later, and it still blows me away. Friends, we have got to continue moving forward in this race. There's a portion of Philippians 3, starting at verse 12, that's titled "Pressing on towards the goal" in my Bible. I want to focus on Philippians 3:12-16 which says,

> I don't mean to say that I have already achieved these things or that I have already reached perfection. But I press on to possess that perfection for which Christ Jesus first possessed me. No, dear brothers and sisters, I have not achieved it, but I focus on this one thing: Forgetting the past and looking forward to what lies ahead, I press on to reach the end of the race and receive the heavenly prize for which God, through Christ Jesus, is calling us.

> Let all who are spiritually mature agree on these things. If you disagree on some point, I believe God will make it plain to you. But we must hold on to the *progress* we have already made. [Emphasis mine.]

Wow! There's so much goodness in this short little passage. Listen, when the enemy presses us, with the end goal being to crush us, we must press and push *forward*! For some of us this is life and death we're talking about here! We must continue on toward the prize. And make no mistake, there *is* a prize at the end. God has a reward for you greater than anything you have ever imagined. He's not dangling a carrot in front of you just so you keep moving. The prize is attainable if you "press on to reach the end of the race."

So, what does pressing on, and not being complacent, look like practically? It can look different given the situation, but here are some real-life steps you can take:

<u>*Stay in the Word.*</u> Keep fueling yourself up on that daily Bread! This year I joined a team of people that decided to read through the Bible in a year. It has been one of the biggest blessings. It always amazes me how often the current day's reading coincides with a challenge I may be facing that week. God is so in the details.

Use the gifts He's blessed you with. Ask Him where you should serve in every season because our gifts are like muscles. The more we use them and work them out, the stronger they get. This serving can be in a church setting but there are many other ways outside of the church to serve as well. I'm part of a church that champions us to go into the world to minister and make a difference. I often ask the Lord for a prophetic word of encouragement for the hostess or waitress when I go out to eat. The response has been such a blessing.

Get accountability. Find people to run this race with. Not yes men! People who champion and love you enough to correct you, motivate you, and keep you in line! They will spur you on to be the best version of yourself ever! I'm so grateful to be surrounded by people who will call me out and say, "You're better than this!" when I get off track.

Stay stationed! Stay faithful to the assignments He's given you and where He's planted you. James 1:12 (NASB) says, "Blessed is a man who perseveres under trial; for once he has been approved, he will receive the crown of life which the Lord has promised to those who love Him." I'm hearing the phrase, "Quitters never prosper." If we live a lifestyle of quitting mid-race, how can we ever expect to win? I experienced a trying job situation as a teenager. In my anger I quit before the Lord gave me the green light to. And guess what happened? I had to retake the "test," if you will. If you quit before God has finished the work He's trying to do in you, you *will* have to retake the test! Let's just say I only had to learn that lesson once.

Walk blameless! Sin begets sin. Drama begets more drama. Sin and drama are heavy weights. Who wants to run with that baggage?

Psalm 15:1-2 says, "Who may worship in your sanctuary, LORD? Who may enter your presence on your holy hill? Those who lead blameless lives and do what is right, speaking the truth from sincere hearts."

Walking or running blamelessly draws us closer to the Lord. Since He's our strength and sustenance for this battle, sign me up!

Those are just a few things I thought of. However, whatever keeps your eyes on the prize … do that! Then do it again! Then keep doing it until you win!

Isolation

The next enemy tactic I want to talk about is isolation. There are many ways the enemy tries to take us out and isolation is definitely one of them. This may be bad news for some of you, but there's no such thing as a Lone Ranger Christian. God designed us for relationship. After all, God is relationship. He's in a relationship with Himself via the Trinity: Father, Son, and Holy Spirit! I know, I know, that's a whole 'nother topic for a whole 'nother day. However, my point is that the Church operates at its best when we are all working together in unison. Let's unpack this a little.

So, I say this all the time: my kid is pretty much me in a little boy's body! LOL. We have pretty much the same personality. He's the life of the party, he's loud like his momma (still working on that inside voice), he's a leader, he talks a lot, and I wouldn't have it any other way. That leadership gift manifests itself in many different ways in him. My least favorite way is when we're with a group of people in public and he takes off in a particular direction ahead of everyone. He's never been the least bit fazed by the fact that he has *no idea* where he's going or where the *group* is trying to go. He just takes the lead.

At least once every time we go to the amusement park I think, "Where is my kid?" The answer is usually about 20 paces ahead of us in the *wrong* direction. Once we find him he gets the same lecture every time. "You have to stay with the rest of the group! We should not have to keep asking where you are!? Why can't you just stay with the rest of us!?" Ahhhhhhhhhhhhh! The frustration! I always have to remind him that kidnappers are looking for the kid who is off by himself. My kid has never met a stranger and trying to explain the concept of "bad people" to a kid like mine is just exhausting sometimes. He loves everyone and thinks everyone is good.

Those chats with him make me think of the analogy of the shepherd and his sheep. I remember learning that predators are always looking for the one sheep who is away from the rest of the flock. They're easier to pick off without a lot of fanfare. That's how our enemy works, too. We were made to live in community. When we pull away for extended periods of time and don't have the friends to hold us accountable, encourage us, and strengthen us, we miss out on being refueled by the rest of the body and reminded why we are essential to the big picture.

Isolation is a trap. The heart of the Father is for us to value our diversity and be as one. One of my favorite passages that expresses His heart on the matter is found in 1 Corinthians 12:12-31 and it's titled in my Bible, "One Body Many Parts." I know you've probably read it a million times. But this time read it while thinking about how the enemy attempts to isolate you from the rest of the body that you are an integral part of.

> The human body has many parts, but the many parts make up one whole body. So it is with the body of Christ. Some of us are Jews, some are Gentiles, some are slaves, and some are free. But we have all been baptized into one body by one Spirit, and we all share the same Spirit.

> Yes, the body has many different parts, not just one part. If the foot says, "I am not a part of the body because I am not a hand," that does not make it any less a part of the body. And if the ear says, "I am not part of the body because I am not an eye," would that make it any less a part of the body? If the whole body were an eye, how would you hear? Or if your whole body were an ear, how would you smell anything?

> But our bodies have many parts, and God has put each part just where he wants it. How strange a body would be if it had only one part! Yes, there are many parts, but only one body. The eye can never say to the hand, "I don't need you." The head can't say to the feet, "I don't need you."

> In fact, some parts of the body that seem weakest and least important are actually the most necessary. And the parts we regard as less honorable are those we clothe with the greatest care. So we carefully protect those parts that should not be seen, while the more honorable parts do not require this special care. So God has put the body together such that extra honor and care are given to those parts that have less dignity. This

makes for harmony among the members, so that all the members care for each other. If one part suffers, all the parts suffer with it, and if one part is honored, all the parts are glad.

All of you together are Christ's body, and each of you is a part of it. Here are some of the parts God has appointed for the church:

> first are apostles,
> second are prophets,
> third are teachers,
> then those who do miracles,
> those who have the gift of healing,
> those who can help others,
> those who have the gift of leadership,
> those who speak in unknown languages.

Are we all apostles? Are we all prophets? Are we all teachers? Do we all have the power to do miracles? Do we all have the gift of healing? Do we all have the ability to speak in unknown languages? Do we all have the ability to interpret unknown languages? Of course not! So you should earnestly desire the most helpful gifts. But now let me show you a way of life that is best of all.

Sometimes it seems people isolate because they feel different. Different is not a bad thing! The enemy tries to convince you that there is something very wrong with you, but the way you were created couldn't be more *right*! As I was writing this I got a vision of a puzzle being put together and at the very end it's discovered that one piece is lost or missing. The puzzle is not complete without it. There's a feeling of loss. Imagine that puzzle piece hiding because it's not like the others. That puzzle piece was intentionally cut differently to serve a different purpose, a specific purpose.

As believers we must understand that the goal isn't to be carbon copies of one another, but instead to complement one another the way we come together and work together. We have different gifts, callings, and purposes by design. Let's celebrate one another and stay in community. We need one other in order to be most effective as the Church.

In the pressing there will be competing voices. There's the enemy's voice and then there's God's voice. I love this quote by Stephen Furtick: "The voice you believe will determine the future you experience."

I feel like the enemy works overtime speaking to us and trying to make us compare our different gifts so we feel lesser than, inadequate, less important, or less integral. The enemy's voice hopes to isolate you and pull you away, making you feel unworthy or less special. In the I Corinthians passage above, Holy Spirit is exhorting you to embrace your differences and to help you believe that you bring something to the table that no other believer does.

You get to choose whose voice you listen to and how you respond to it. Please do not make the mistake of missing out on your purpose and destiny because you were hoodwinked into backing yourself into a corner. A corner of isolation.

Isolation is the opposite of what the Father desires for you. I know many of you can probably attest to making at least one poor decision and in retrospect wish you would have bounced the decision off of someone first. Or maybe you had a friend who was able to free you from the grip of depression and negative thought patterns by simply helping you talk things out. I've heard of people who testified that serving in some capacity (volunteering anywhere) helped shift their mood and enable them to focus on the bigger picture. We were not built to do life alone. If you struggle with friendships, I challenge you to ask God to send you some kingdom friendships. Ask him to highlight some people you can reach out to. Come out of the cave of isolation today.

There are many forms of pressing that I have not mentioned. Rejection, complacency and isolation are just of few that I have personally experienced or seen operating up close and personal in other people's lives. There are many more like comparison, generational curses, health issues, financial trouble, turmoil in relationships, delay of God's promises, disappointment, and injustice. No matter the tactic, our primary strategy must be to press in closer to God. Every one of the enemy's tactics is designed to pull you away from the Shepherd and away from your calling. Be alert and be on the lookout! Stay in the Word and stay in community. Perseverance is the name of the game. Be steadfast, my friends. Make the enemy rue the day he ever decided to mess with you!

You are more than a conqueror. Whatever you are currently battling is your authority in the making. Jesus died, rose again, and took back the keys of hell. He now has authority over death and hell. Whatever battle you are fighting, you are getting the keys of authority to overcome it in your own life and then to help others overcome it.

Over the course of my various battles I would hear a common thread through all my prophetic words. Minister after pastor after prophet would tell me that what I was going through was in order to help those coming after me. If I can be 100% honest with you, some days that would encourage me and other days it would actually trigger me. LOL! I would ask the Lord why I was selected to be the forerunner. Why was I the one who had to breakthrough for the others behind me? On some really bad days I asked where were the ones that were supposed to be ahead of me, carving the path for me? Regardless of God's response, I gave Him the strongest "yes" I could muster. I tell Him on a regular basis that He has my "yes" no matter what.

I trust Him and I invite you to lay down all the fears, silence all the voices that are not from Him, and give Him your "yes". Set your face like flint like it says in Isaiah 50:7 (NIV), "Because the Sovereign LORD helps me, I will not be disgraced. Therefore have I set my face like flint, and I know I will not be put to shame" The NLT version even adds, "Therefore, I have set my face like a stone, *determined to do his will*. And I know that I will not be put to shame."

May we be determined to do His will even in the pressing. For we can be confident He will give us the victory and our reward will be incredible.

CHAPTER 18

Not Crushed

I'm in awe as I write the final words in this book. I'm so honored that God would even call me to write it, honestly. So many times, in the midst of these battles, we wonder why? What's the purpose? What is this unto? Why me? Why now? Again? I'm not going to even presume to know the answer to any of those questions. With this finite mind of mine, I'm not even going to attempt to figure it out or even question God about every detail. We all see how that worked out for Job, haha! I lost count of how many times I've said, "Behold God is great and I do not know Him" (Job 26:36).

What I will say is this: I have observed and fully experienced the truths of Genesis 50:20, which says in the NLT version, "You intended to harm me, but God intended it all for good. He brought me to this position so I could save the lives of many people."

Over the years, I've come to realize the impact of just sharing my stories in casual conservation with people in my life. God has used those random testimonies to help and encourage others. Just like He's used the stories of others to spark me into greater faith or action.

I recently received a random text from a new friend. A mutual friend connected us due to some shared business interests. We had texted a few times over a year ago, then met in person a few months later. However, we never had a chance to connect again. I was surprised to randomly receive this text from her. She seemed very adamant that we should connect over coffee very soon. I was positive she must have something important to tell me. As we sat down for coffee that week, she shared how God brought me to her mind and she just knew we needed to connect. I'm thinking, "Interesting." As we start catching up, I feel a nudging in my spirit to share a testimony in the making that I had been keeping very private for over six months. Up until that point, only a few other very close friends knew what was happening. And even they didn't have all the details. So when I felt this prompting, I simply stepped out in obedience and spilled the beans.

She was on the edge of her seat as I shared the latest walk of faith God had me on. As I concluded my story with the cliffhanger I was currently in, she opened up and shared some private things about herself. Apparently, God was inviting her on the same exact journey He'd started me on back in December of 2019! She could not believe that I had walked, and was still walking, through the same bizarre set of circumstances she was in the midst of! At one point she shouted, "I knew there was a reason I was supposed to connect with you immediately!" We both laughed. She had felt there was an urgency for us to connect. Now she understood why. We both left that coffee shop more in awe of God than we were when we arrived. I felt completely refreshed and I'm sure she did too.

A few weeks after our coffee date she sent me a text sharing how my story encouraged her to take a huge leap of faith and go hard after what God was calling her to.

Revelation 12:11 (NASB) reminds us that, "… they overcame him because of the blood of the Lamb and because of the word of their testimony … ." I want to encourage you that there is so much power in *your testimony!* In this one example, the enemy was trying to keep my new friend trapped in a prison of fear and intimidation concerning this next step toward her destiny. However, the testimony of what God was doing in my life unlocked her and set her free to pursue it with everything she had.

Many times the enemy will try to keep us trapped in a place of shame, embarrassment, or fear so we don't share what seems like a "trivial" or "unimportant" testimony. The story I shared with her was very vulnerable. I imagined her response was going to be something along the lines of, "That's crazy, girl! Have fun with that!" or "That makes no sense. Are you sure this is God?" Or maybe the enemy was just trying to convince me that's the way she was going to respond in order to stop me from sharing. You see, the enemy knows your story is the key to setting someone else free from their own personal hell or prison. So he'll try to keep you silent at every turn.

In this book, I was very intentional about sharing some wins, some epic fails, and some testimonies that are still in the making. We are all a work in progress. Just remember, if you don't quit, you will win.

God's heart is to give you "... a crown of beauty for ashes, a joyous blessing instead of mourning, festive praise instead of despair" (Isaiah 61:3).

Those areas of your life that seem destroyed beyond repair are actually primed for the redemptive, restorative work of the Father. There is hope! Every pressing and attack from the enemy comes with the opportunity to learn more about ourselves and to strengthen ourselves in the Lord. As a matter of fact, I love how the enemy will sometimes overplay his hand. A lot of times his attack results in catapulting me into a new season of victory. Yeah. Take that, sucker! I believe you will experience the same thing in your walk as you lean into God as your source and strength.

So full disclosure, I'm horrible when it comes to ending conversations and this book is no exception. I could go on forever boasting about my God and cheering you on to accomplish all He has given you to accomplish. For those of you who currently find yourselves in the thick of an epic battle, I leave you with Hebrews 4:16, "So let us come boldly to the throne of our gracious God. There we will receive his mercy, and we will find grace to help us when we need it most."

We may be pressed, my friends, but we are most certainly not crushed. Your victory is closer than you think and heaven is planning the party!

I'll see you on the frontlines as we keep pressing forward!

RESOURCES

Books:
Keep Your Love On – Danny Silk
Good or God – John Bevere
The Attributes of God – A.W. Tozer
Prayer Rain – Dr. Olukoya

Music:
"Put on Christ" by Laura Hackett – https://youtu.be/XLfKVv1JrKY
"This is Me" Greatest Showman Soundtrack – https://youtu.be/CjxugyZCfuw
"Lord You're Holy" by Eddie James – https://www.youtube.com/
    watch?v=outREf1Po_g
"Holy" by Matt Gilman – https://www.youtube.com/watch?v=5JGaAkW5Rpc
"Better Word" by Leeland – https://www.youtube.com/
    watch?v=MOgYFwFemB0

Teachers:
Katie Souza (Soul Healing) – https://katiesouza.com

Ministries:
Deliverance – Bear Creek Ministries – http://www.bcrcamp.com
Glory of Zion Ministries – https://gloryofzion.org
Inner Healing – Bethel SOZO – http://bethelsozo.com
Riverstone Church SOZO – https://riverstoneonline.org/ministries/sozo/

Movies:
The Greatest Showman 2017
Pitch Perfect 3

About the Author

Cassandra Bellevue was born in Port-au-Pince, Haiti. She was raised in Philadelphia, and although she currently resides in Atlanta, she's still hanging on tight to her Yankee roots.

Cassandra was saved at the age of 16 through an incredible encounter with God and hasn't looked back. Through her walk with God, she discovered her identity in Christ and the prophetic call on her life. Later, the Lord launched Cassandra into marketplace ministry, leading Bible studies and mentoring coworkers. She could also be found mentoring high school girls at the church she attended. Between the marketplace ministry and mentoring high school girls, she discovered the joy and passion of championing others into their destiny.

Cassandra currently serves as a prophetic ministry leader and worship team leader at her church. She has a heart to speak God's words of encouragement over His people and sing prophetically during worship. After surviving many difficult tests and trials, she has become even more passionate about equipping others to wage war against the plans, schemes, and plots of the enemy.

Cassandra has a son, Joshua, AKA "the most amazing kid in the world," who she also claims is the "funniest person on the planet." She attests that Mom is the best thing anyone has ever called her. Cassandra's hobbies include traveling, catching shows and musicals at the theater, taking dance lessons, attending outdoor festivals, and listening to live music. A few of her bucket list items include visiting Salzburg, Austria, to relive some of the scenes from her favorite movie, "The Sound of Music," writing music for recording artists, and entering a ballroom dancing competition.

To keep up with Cassandra's itinerary, to book for speaking engagements and/or see the latest merchandise, you can visit her website at www.BellevueProduction.co. You can also follow her on Youtube and/or Instagram: @CassandraBellevue.

Shannon,

Thank you for all that you do with our kiddos and your extra help w/ Joshua this year!

When I asked Joshua what he wanted to get his teachers he said: "YOUR BOOK!" LoL

I pray that you encounter the heart of the Father as you read through it. Merry Christmas!

Cassandra Bellfield ♡